CW01677089

To John

a very happy birthday.

Desmond.

1975.

The Sporting Empress

Also by John Welcome

THE CHELTENHAM GOLD CUP
CHEATING AT CARDS, THE CASES IN COURT
FRED ARCHER, HIS LIFE AND TIMES
NECK OR NOTHING. THE LIFE
AND TIMES OF BOB SIEVIER
THE WELCOME COLLECTION

The Sporting Empress

THE STORY OF ELIZABETH OF AUSTRIA
AND BAY MIDDLETON

JOHN WELCOME

Michael Joseph London

First published in Great Britain by MICHAEL JOSEPH LTD
52 Bedford Square London WC1B 3EF
1975

ISBN 0 7181 1323 3

Photoset and printed
in Great Britain by
REDWOOD BURN LIMITED
Trowbridge & Esher
in Eleven on Twelve point Baskerville
on paper supplied by P.F. Bingham Ltd

Contents

Illustration acknowledgements

Grateful acknowledgement is made of permission to reproduce illustrations as follows: The Mansell Collection for the cartoon of Lord Spencer, de Grimm's picture of Elizabeth, *Vanity Fair's* picture of Bay Middleton, and Elizabeth hunting with the Meath; Radio Times Hulton Picture Library for the pictures of Elizabeth at the time of her betrothal, and Count Charles Kinsky; *Country Life* for photographs of Easton Neston and Cottesbrooke; Mrs B. J. Fowler for the photograph of Summerhill; the Borwick collection for photographs of Bay Middleton and the Hohenembs Cup.

Illustrations

Foreword

I wish to express my gratitude for the gracious permission of Her Majesty the Queen to make use of material from the Royal Archives and to quote from it. I should also like to pay tribute to the courtesy and assistance I received throughout the research for this book from Mr Robert Mackworth-Young, the Librarian, Windsor Castle, and his Registrar Miss Jane Langton.

My sincere thanks are also due to two experts on the period, Mr Edward Crankshaw and Miss Joan Haslip. Miss Haslip encouraged me from the outset, for I spoke to her when the book was in its birth throes as it were, and she has kindly given me permission to use quotes from her book *The Lonely Empress*. I owe Mr Crankshaw an especial debt not only for his own assistance in answering my queries but also for introducing me to Prince Alfons Clary who was indefatigable in putting at my disposal his personal knowledge of the period and in answering the many letters with which I bombarded him. He and the Princess were kindness itself when I visited them in their flat on the Zattere, providing me with hospitality and replying to my many questions with patience, accuracy and charm. I wish to put on record my gratitude to them for giving me so generously of their memories and recollections, thus supplying me with material I could never have obtained elsewhere.

A special note of thanks must go to Mrs Mary Fowler of Rahinstown, for information and introductions and for the assistance she rendered throughout the research, to Colonel Michael Borwick, and Colonel Peter Borwick, Bay Middleton's grandsons, and Mrs Cicely Borwick, who were all kind enough to lend their help and to provide illustrations from the family collection. Mrs Gwynneth Lloyd gave me invaluable family recollections of the Empress and her retinue in Cheshire and details of her routine and accoutrements on a hunting morning.

I must mention with thanks, too, the information and help given by Nicholas Morrogh Ryan and Mrs King, Leonard Morrogh's grandchildren; R. W. McKeever who unearthed other original sources for me; the late Captain D. A. R. Baggallay who, as always, was helpfulness itself in searching records and giving of his time, and who loaned me a hunting map of Meath made at the time of the Empress's first visit; R. G. Leonard who gave so generously of his vast knowledge of hunting in Meath and loaned me hunting diaries of the time; Nesbit Waddington for his help about the Linde visit; Lady Violet Powell for the Warwickshire story; Mr A. R. Eager of the Royal Dublin Society Library and the Librarian of the London Library for searching out source books for me; and Mr Seumas Galvin and Dr D. J. K. McCarthy for lending me books I could not otherwise have obtained.

Quotations are made from *The Letters of Queen Victoria*, Second Series, Volume II by kind permission of John Murray (Publishers) Ltd, and from *Dearest Mama* by Roger Fulford, by kind permission of Evans Brothers Ltd.

I must also thank the Superintendent of the Hofburg who received me with such courtesy at very short notice and went to great pains to help, as did two guides in the Hofburg and the Schönbrunn whose names I have unfortunately mislaid but to whom I pay belated thanks.

Finally, Mrs Joan Saunders of the Writer's and Artist's Research has given invaluable help in all my books, but this time she has really excelled even her own former endeavours. In seeking out and unearthing hunting and other reports in contemporary papers obscure and otherwise and supplying me with them she enabled me to trace almost day by day the movements of the Empress and all the chief characters in this story throughout their visits. It was a monumental task splendidly performed and I can only once more repeat my thanks to her for fulfilling it.

I must add that the opinions expressed about any of the characters in the book are my own alone and should in no way be identified with all or any of those mentioned above who were so helpful to me in my search for material.

J. W.

The Sporting Empress

CHAPTER ONE

Sisi

'If we had not been born princes we would have been circus-riders.' So spoke Duke Max in Bavaria, 'The Good Duke Max', to his daughter Elizabeth, the future Empress when, as a girl, he had praised her for her riding of one of his young horses.

'The Good Duke Max' was a descendant of the House of Wittelsbach, which had provided the hereditary rulers of Bavaria for over seven hundred years. It became the smart thing to say in England later that all the Wittelsbachs were mad. They were not mad nor anything like it, but they were cultured and artistic, dreamers not doers, romantics not practical men of affairs. A strong strain of eccentricity, sometimes wilful, did, however, run right through the family and its lineage, and Max had more than his share of it. With neither great possessions nor responsibilities to cumber his tastes but with enough wealth to indulge them, he gave them free rein. They were: horses, women, music (especially the zither which he played extremely well), books and the circus, in roughly that order.

The unwilling subject of a marriage of convenience at the age of twenty to his second counsin Ludovica, the ambitious daughter of King Maximilian's second marriage, he never permitted the bonds of matrimony to interfere with the enjoyment of his favourite pursuits. She, for her part, was equally disappointed in being married off by her parents, as she thought, beneath her. A story persisted in the family that, after the marriage service, whilst on the way to their bedroom, she tricked him into entering one of the empty cells of the converted nunnery of Tegernsee that served as a palace, turned the key in the lock and left him there.

After this cold and solitary wedding night the Duke trod his own wayward path, but he did at least purchase for his family the castle and estate of Possenhofen, some miles from Munich. Set in a wonderful country of mountains and lakes, this had appealed to his romantic eye. He could not have made a better choice and all the family loved 'Possi' throughout their lives, returning to it again and again as a refuge from the world outside.

There were eight of them in all, each almost casually begotten by him on the body of his wife during his infrequent visits to the castle. A traveller, a dreamer, a poet *manqué,* a sort of Byron without either the caddishness or the genius, he went on long journeys, conducted love affairs, set up literary and drinking circles, wandered about incognito with circuses and gave displays of *haute école* in the riding school of his Munich Palace before selected and indeed unselected guests. If he had any politics at all he was a liberal. He sympathised with Hungarian aspirations and one of his circle, Count John Majlath, a Hungarian, was the first to inspire in Elizabeth romantic ideals about Hungary and its people which were to have their full flowering later on.

A wholly engaging character, Duke Max was greatly loved by everyone except his wife. There was no trace in him of either pomposity or pretension. Much later, when his daughter had become Empress and was visiting Possenhofen with a suite composed largely of Austrian nobility hand-picked by her mother-in-law from the highest court circles, he casually asked two of the grandest amongst them if they would care to make up a four at billiards with himself and his gamekeeper. It was not surprising that the children, though they saw little of him, loved what they saw. They were provided, too, with everything they could want to enable them to take part in country pursuits. The stables were thronged with horses, and they were good horses, chosen with care by a man who knew what he was doing, for he was determined that none of his children would disgrace him in the saddle. To teach the girls balance he had the pommels of their side saddles made so as to be interchangeable: they rode first on one side and then on the other. He also made them ride without stirrups, an innovation in teaching at that time, and to go over small jumps without the assistance of stirrup or leathers. Of all the children it was his second daughter, born on 24 December 1837 and christened Elizabeth after her Godmother Queen Elizabeth of Prussia, but known always in the family as 'Sisi', who inherited most of his skill.

Sisi had hands of gossamer and an instinctive sympathy for the animal she was riding. Horses sensed this and throughout her life they went kindly for her. 'She has the knack', Franz Jebhart, the instructor of *haute école* at Vienna, wrote later on, 'of putting herself into immediate and almost mesmeric communication with her horse. She far outshines any rider of her own sex that I have seen.' That knack was partly inherited from her father and partly taught by him.

She was the closest among the family to her father personally and the nearest to him in temperament. But whereas his appears to have been a happy disposition, by some quirk of heredity and interbreeding hers was not. She was almost pathologically shy and, as in the case of so many shy people, was also abnormally sensitive, 'born with a skin too few'. She sensed criticism where none was intended and reacted to it in an exaggerated manner. Human contacts, save amongst the very few chosen by her for their sympathy or charm, were anathema to her. It was to animals that she turned in her childhood and throughout her life. She deeply and truly loved animals and understood them in the manner of many over-complicated people who find human relationships with their day-to-day balance and counter-balance of stress and strain too difficult to cope with. In the famous equestrian portrait of her painted for the Emperor at the time of her engagement, when she was not quite sixteen, there can be discerned about the mouth a withdrawn, almost sly look which hints at nervous trouble later on. It was not a false hint and that nervous trouble was to haunt and torture her throughout her tragic life.

Had she been a plain woman or indeed even possessed of something less than the breath-taking loveliness that was given to her she might have passed her life just as her father did, away from the world's stares, at Possenhofen with her horses and her dogs, her friends and her books. But beauty was given to her and brought her no peace.

She was not particularly pretty as a child. Those who

remembered her when she was young recalled a round-faced, quite unexceptional little girl with amber eyes and bad teeth. It was these teeth which brought about her first clash with her future mother-in-law, who was also her mother's sister, the domineering Archduchess Sophie. The outspoken Archduchess told Ludovica in her daughter's presence that Sisi had bad teeth and should take better care of them. The girl, who was just growing into adolescence and consciousness of her appearance, resented the brusque remark. On this occasion her sensitivity to criticism had at least some justification for the Archduchess persisted in repeating it. Indeed she brought up the question of Sisi's bad teeth with Franz Joseph when he told her of his choice. As a result he wrote to his mother shortly afterwards: 'The next time you meet Sisi you will find her teeth are quite white.' This was the blindness of love, for her bad teeth remained with her all her life as the only blemish on her beauty.

Ever afterwards, because of these criticisms, Sisi drew her upper lip over her teeth when speaking and scarcely opened her mouth. This made much of what she said quite inaudible and led to some ludicrous situations at Court later on. The Crown Princess of Germany writing to her mother Queen Victoria described the experience of a 'gentleman who was very deaf' on being presented to her shortly after her accession. 'She said: "Are you married?" The man answered "Sometimes." The Empress said "Have you any children?" and the luckless man bawled out "At times!"'

Despite the teeth, by the time she was approaching sixteen she had become a raging beauty. She had sprung up suddenly as children will; she was lissom; she had coils of wonderful auburn hair; her amber eyes glowed with youth and freshness; her complexion was flawless. In a word, she was captivating and in a few short months she was to find at her feet the most powerful monarch in Europe.

It was not designed to happen that way at all.

In 1848 the Austrian Empire was rocking. There was open rebellion in Italy and Hungary; revolution raged through the streets of Vienna and the court had to flee to Innsbruck. It became apparent that the Emperor Ferdinand, weak, incompetent, and indecisive, could no longer control the march of events. But the Archduchess Sophie, 'the only man in the Hofburg', had plans to restore the situation. The Archduchess's husband Franz Karl, like Duke Max, was more interested in horses and dogs than in politics and power. He was as ill-suited as his brother to take the throne in a moment of crisis. The Archduchess, surveying the situation with an eye accustomed to command, knew that there was only one course to be taken if the Empire was to be saved. She herself had dearly wished to be Empress; indeed it was the greatest ambition of a life in which power had taken the place of love. With immense strength of will and character she sacrificed that ambition to what she considered to be the greater good of the dynasty and the nation. The Emperor Ferdinand was forced to abdicate; Franz Karl was passed over as if he did not exist; Franz Joseph, eldest son of the Archduchess and Franz Karl, was proclaimed Emperor at the age of eighteen.

It was a bleak inheritance to accept. The radicals, led by Kossuth, were in control in Hungary; the rising in Italy was only just being contained by the army; at home there was ferment and unrest. Violence seemed everywhere unleashed. When warned of his fate the young Emperor-elect had a last 'bear-fight' or rough and tumble with his brothers. Then, saying 'farewell my youth', he went to his mother to accept her dictation and his responsibilities.

The Archduchess hated the Hungarians. She regarded them, it has been said, as the Irish of the Empire, a wild, unbiddable, trouble-making people. With the aid of the Russians the insurrection was ruthlessly and savagely suppressed. The Minister President Count Louis Batthany was executed despite the strongest pleas for his reprieve. Kossuth and Count Julius Andrassy, a young member of a leading Hungarian family who had espoused the Radical cause, were fortunate to escape into exile with their lives. The army was purged and thirteen generals said to have taken part in the uprising were shot. Though done in the name of the Emperor, this was mainly the work of the Archduchess, fostered and encouraged by Prince Felix Schwarzenberg, the political architect of the new Austria. It was to have an incalculable effect on the future life of Franz Joseph and on his marriage.

The army held Italy; order was restored; the Archduchess was Emperor in all but name. Gradually stability of a sort crept back to all the vast dominions. It was then time, the Archduchess thought, to look about for a suitable wife for her son.

The Archduchess knew all too clearly that the peace she had restored might well prove illusory. Underneath the iron grip established by her and the Adjutant-General, the ambitious and ruthless Count Grunne, discontent still seethed. Kossuth was in England, so her secret police told her, plotting his return and attempting to involve in his plans Count Andrassy, who had also found refuge there, so as to bind the aristocracy to his schemes for renewing the revolt. Beyond the Alps the Italians were only waiting for the first sign of weakness to burst into open rebellion. If she could secure Bavaria by ties of blood she would have both a bastion and a bridgehead to cope with any threat to the Empire's southern flank. The means of doing this lay ready to her hand in the shape of her sister Ludovica's family and more especially the eldest daughter of that family, Helene, known to them all as Nene.

Nene was a dark-haired, quiet, serious girl, malleable and sensible. She was, the Archduchess thought, excellent material for an Empress, and she would be as clay in her hands. A meeting was arranged to take place at Ischll, the summer residence of the Imperial family, between the Archduchess and Franz Joseph on the one side and the Duchess Ludovica with Princess Helene on the other.

The Good Duke Max was not included in the Duchess's party for he was away on one of his escapades but, more or less by chance, Sisi, the girl-child, was separated from her dogs and her horses and brought along too. She was wayward, shy and hesitant in company but it should have been obvious to everyone, had they not been so preoccupied in preparing for the great event, that her beauty had begun its flowering and that she far surpassed her elder sister in looks and, above all, in that indefinable human quality which we call charm.

On the afternoon of 15 August 1853 the two girls were brought in to the formal drawing room at Ischll and presented to the Emperor. Throughout the whole of his long life Franz Joseph could never resist a pretty face. Had he done so in that instant of time in the great drawing room at Ischll, the history of the Habsburg Empire and indeed of the world might have been very different. For there can be no question but that Helene with her serious mind, her mental stability, her willingness to accept and not rebel against circumstances, was far better fitted to be Empress than her lovely sister. As it was, however, Franz Joseph took one look at Sisi and thereafter his eyes never left her. Her freshness and beauty captivated him immediately, and he fell in love. In that moment he condemned them both and many others to a lifetime of unhappiness.

They were married on 24 April 1854, when Sisi had just passed her sixteenth birthday.

The intervening period had not been without its difficulties. Franz Joseph's life was governed by routine. He was humourless, over-conscientious and a slave to his desk. He had been called too soon to his high estate and his responsibilities sat heavily upon him. Combined with this he had a tremendous feeling for the realities both of position and power. He was a Habsburg, heir to six hundred years of pomp, privilege and the almost divine right to rule. He brought a presence with him on all occasions, an aura of 'the All-Highest' for, young as he was, it had been instilled into him that he had been born to rule, and rule he would and did. Thus he found it difficult to unbend, and the informalities of Possenhofen when he stayed there with his betrothed were strange and slightly shocking to him.

One thing that brought them together and solved for the moment all their difficulties was their common love of horses. Horsemanship had not come naturally to him as it had to her. But dedication and hard work under the tuition of the best riding masters, provided for him by his mother, had made him into a competent and polished rider. He was very proud of this achievement and delighted when Bismarck, a year or so earlier, wrote of him: 'The Hungarians are enthusiastic about his natural pronunciation of their language and the elegance of his horsemanship.' Since at that time the Hungarians detested him almost as much as he distrusted them, and since they ranked horsemanship highest of manly achievements, this was praise indeed.

On the long rides they took alone together through the beautiful countryside surrounding Possenhofen, he became almost a boy again. Having said farewell to his youth some years ago he found himself regaining it in the person of this enchanting and vibrant child he had captured. She, on the other hand, was even then beginning to wonder if she was throwing away hers. It was only a few months later that she was scribbling in her commonplace book one of those immature verses in which all her life she tried to give expression to her true feelings.

> I waken from a vision rich
> Wherein my spirit captive lay
> And vainly curse the hour in which
> Freedom! I gambled thee away!

The protracted marriage ceremonies were a torture to her. During these long drawn-out formalities her innate shyness and dislike of public demonstrations took possession of her and did not improve either her temper or her moods. 'On show like a freak in a circus,' she grumbled to her mother as she was entering the State coach for the ceremonial drive to Vienna. In fact it was Renz, the circus rider, who gave her the only few moments of enjoyment she had throughout the long, boring and exhausting ceremonies which left her limp physically, depressed in mind and longing for the simplicities of 'dear Possi'. Renz, who was a friend of her father's, knew of her fondness for horses and the circus. The show took place five days after the actual wedding ceremony. Renz with twelve greys and eleven blacks gave a dazzling display in her honour ending with an exhibition of *haute école* by himself on an Arab. She clapped her hands in delight as he left the arena. 'It really was too lovely!' she said. 'I must get to know that man.' It was not a remark likely to endear her to her mother-in-law.

The marriage itself had been consummated two days earlier. The sexual relations between Franz Joseph and his young bride have given rise to much speculation and it seems certain that they, or perhaps the lack of them, hold the key to much of what was to happen later to this ill-matched Imperial pair. Did they consist of demand on the one side and acquiescence on the other—the pattern of many marriages, Imperial and otherwise, then and always? Or did she urgently reciprocate the sexual drive and ardour he unquestionably possessed?

The answer almost certainly is that she was never truly sexually awakened during the whole span of her life. On that wedding night she was sixteen, shy to extremes and unconscious as yet of the power and allure her beauty would give her. Despite the louche atmosphere of the Bavarian court and the knowledge she must have gained of her father's flagrant infidelities, she was still innocent in the absolute sense of the word and totally without the knowledge that would have enabled her to come to terms with the ceremonial surrounding an Imperial consummation.

The story of his sudden appearance before her on their wedding night in his full regimentals and his ceremonial discarding of them to her ultimate horror may perhaps be discounted since it has been told in different versions about many crowned heads. What is certain, however, is that the Archduchess insisted and he acquiesced in the full observation of the brutal family custom whereby the bride was produced for inspection, as it were, before the household at breakfast the following morning. It was one of the many things for which she never forgave the Archduchess Sophie.

Much has been made of the antipathy between the Archduchess and the niece who became her daughter-in-law. That it existed and quickly turned to a bitter loathing on the part of the Empress cannot be denied. From the first they were utterly incompatible. The Archduchess was a slave to duty and convention. To these twin idols she had sacrificed the greatest ambition of her life—to become Empress and rule in name as well as in fact. Now she saw herself supplanted by a mere child, a 'romp' as she had once termed her daughter-in-law, who cared for none of these things. The Empress indeed displayed no interest in either power or politics; she hated ceremonial, was openly bored at state balls and could not countenance the hidebound society of the Viennese court which was ruled in its entirety by protocol and convention. Her only ambition, the Archduchess sourly noted, appeared to be to escape to the stables.

Elizabeth for her part was unquestionably too sensitive of the Archduchess's overbearing methods. She was prepared to overlook no slight, however small or indeed imaginary, to forget nothing and to forgive nothing. Like her father she longed to form her own suite, to break away from the strait-lacing of convention and to have about her only those whom she liked, from whatever strata of society they came. But the Archduchess, wisely from her own point of view, insisted on reserving to herself the right to make the appointments to the Empress's household. The people nominated by her came from the oldest and soundest of families, and were trusted adherents of hers who could be relied upon to serve her interests if they were ever to be at variance with those of their Imperial mistress.

Franz Joseph did not interfere. Apart from being afraid of his mother, he was almost overborne by the appalling problems of autocratic government. Grappling with these took up all his attention to the exclusion of his personal feelings and his private life. In fact Franz Joseph adored his 'Sisi', as he invariably called her, and was to continue to do so until the end of his long life. But it was an adoration which found too little expression. He could not, or would not, find the time to be with her; he was driven by devils different from hers, being those concerned with the exercise of power and the application of his every effort towards it. When they were alone together the task of interpreting her moods and fancies was quite beyond him for he had neither imagination nor compassion. But at least when he was there he was a bulwark against the forces of the 'Court camarilla' which she felt were ranged against her.

The grave illness of her first child, Sophie, in 1857 while she was away in Hungary, followed by the child's death, was a terrible blow. In her grief she withdrew from society altogether, changed her apartments in the Hofburg and would allow only the Emperor to approach her. The birth of an heir, Rudolph, in the following year did little to console her. And then the Emperor went away to the wars to take personal command of the campaign against the French in Italy.

Alone again, despair and melancholy possessed her more strongly than ever. There can, however, be little doubt that much of her loneliness was of her own making. Instead of trying at least to some extent to mollify the old nobility and to seek out those who might be sympathetic to her, she displayed her distaste for them quite openly. Her beauty and charm could have won her friends and companions from amongst them but she threw these gifts away. Moreover she was indiscreet, for when she mocked them for their grandeur and pretensions she did so openly, not caring who heard. She had all her father's irreverence for rank and much of his wit and there was no lack of willing tongues ready to repeat her sayings where they would hurt the most. The barriers of mutual dislike between the court and herself grew broader and more unsurmountable. Suddenly, with the Emperor's absence, she felt herself beset by enemies and at their mercy. She wrote him long, eager letters imploring his permission to be with him in the camp. There she felt—and she was probably right, as subsequent events were to show—she could have lived the life she loved. There would be action, horses, excitement, all the things she thrived on. Above all she would be away from the stultifying court ceremonial, the whispering courtiers and the strictures of the Archduchess.

But practical considerations, as always, prevailed with Franz Joseph. He wrote back stiffly: 'For the present, unfortunately, I cannot comply with your wish, though I should love to beyond words,' and he could not refrain from adding the homily which must have infuriated her: 'Women are out of place in the disturbed life at Headquarters and I cannot set my army a bad example.'

Now she had only herself to turn to and she had not the mental resources to withstand the twin pressures of loneliness and unhappiness. She began to suffer the first of the attacks of nervous melancholia which were to plague her for the rest of her life. She fled from the summer palace of Schönbrunn, which she disliked only a little less than the gloomy Hofburg, to Laxenburg, an Imperial summer palace just outside Vienna where at least there were woods and flowers, rivers and lakes. But the melancholia did not lift. She believed herself, with some truth, to be entirely alone and friendless in a world and a society which she hated. She suspected, too, that the Archduchess was using the secret police to report on her movements, her attitudes and her health. In this she may have been right for Seeburger, her doctor, an appointee of the Archduchess whom Elizabeth distrusted and disliked, did make a report to the Head of Police in which he said: 'I find her lacking both as an Empress and a wife. She has nothing to do yet she goes out riding for hours on end, ruining her health. An icy gulf separates her from the Archduchess Sophie.'

So far from ruining her health it was in fact only her horses and her riding which kept her sane. Through them, too, she found a new friend. Henry Holmes, an Englishman, had charge of the Imperial riding horses. He was one of the many English grooms and horsemen of one sort or another who sought and found employment in Austria and Hungary during those years. 'Dear Holmes' was a born horseman who loved his charges and cared for them. He had, like the Empress, beautiful hands and an instinctive sympathy with animals. She went riding with him and discovered in him a silent understanding which gave her at least some of the reassurance she so badly needed. He became her inseparable companion on their daily rides. This was duly reported to the Archduchess who in turn conveyed her strongest disapproval to the Emperor. The unfortunate Franz Joseph, with his armies falling to pieces around him, worn out by the strains of an unsuccessful campaign, worried about his wife's health and longing to see her again, found himself bombarded by the Archduchess with this piece of domestic triviality. But once again he showed that however much he loved his wife he could not understand her character. His reaction was stiff and unsympathetic. 'I have thought over the question of your riding', he wrote, 'and I cannot allow you to ride alone with Holmes, for it is not proper.'

She was as wilful as he was uncomprehending. She disregarded his instructions and continued to scandalise society and the Archduchess by giving herself the small solace of the Englishman's companionship. They rode out together until the Emperor's return. She even persuaded Holmes to begin to teach her to jump. He put up a few hurdles in the park at Laxenburg and, after carefully schooling the horses himself, allowed her to pop over them. It brought a breath of excitement into her life but it gave open scandal at court.

The Emperor came back from the war in the summer of 1859. They were reunited and at first all appeared well between them. Certainly there were no recriminations on his part. But the aftermath of a nervous crisis still had her in its grip. It is possible also that she may not have been sufficiently ardent in her sexual embraces for a man returning from battle worn and harried and looking for the solaces of the flesh, for something at all events went disastrously wrong. There were stories at court of infidelities discreetly conducted. If she heard them the blow to her pride and affront to her beauty must have been traumatic. Then she became aware of symptoms of illness within herself. A peculiar swelling appeared on her wrists and ankles and 'an unsightly rash broke out on Her Majesty's face'. She also complained of sore throats. The hated Seeburger was called in and prescribed binding silver coins round her affected joints. This completely failed to effect any cure. In a succession of stormy scenes she managed to have Seeburger dismissed but his successor, Skoda, was no better. It was announced that she was suffering from a possible tubercular affection of her throat which could spread to her lungs.

No one has adequately or accurately diagnosed the true nature of the Empress's illness but one thing is certain that, whatever it was, it was not what it was officially announced to be. There were murmurs then and have been ever since that the Emperor had infected her with one or other form of venereal disease. It is said, in fact, that the report of Dr Fischer (the Wittelsbach family physician who was later called in) which was lost or destroyed along with many other of the Habsburg archives in the Second World War, pointed unmistakably to this. All the known symptoms—the swellings at the ankle and wrist, the rash, the sore throats—indicate the accuracy of this diagnosis.

It must be said, however, that the stories of a venereal infection which were current at court even if exchanged only in whispers were totally discounted by those then close to the Emperor and Empress and still are by their descendants. It was and is maintained by them that the cloak of mystery with which Fischer surrounded the disease and his treatment of it was responsible for much of the speculation and for the wilder theories that followed it.

Fischer was neither liked nor accepted by the members of Viennese high society. Naturally enough, too, he was cordially hated by the Empress's discarded doctors, who criticised his methods and branded him a quack. A ludicrous incident that occurred shortly after his arrival in Vienna was widely quoted to discredit him and to hold him up as a figure of no consequence.

Fischer was a keen shot and one of his ambitions was to shoot a Viennese stag. Stags and almost every other sort of wild game inhabited in profusion the Danube marshes to the south of the city. One day Fischer decided to take time off from his duties in order to seek out and kill a stag. Unknown to him there were stags in the Prater also. These animals, however, were all but tame. They were fed by visitors and would approach their carriages as they drove through the park. Great favourites with the nobility and gentry, some of them almost became pets, having names conferred on them and being paid special attentions.

As the carriage bearing Fischer to the shooting grounds was traversing the Prater one of these stags, an elderly, affable animal who was universally loved, approached it, expecting the usual attentions from its occupant. Mistaking him for his quarry, Fischer shot him dead.

The story flew round Vienna and Fischer immediately became an object of contempt and derision, especially in Society. He was cut dead by the court and his carriage was actually booed in the streets. Those who wished to defend the honour of the Emperor and Empress used—and still use—the incident to dismiss Fischer as a charlatan. He may well have been one. Certainly his treatment was little more successful in restoring the Empress to health than that of his discarded predecessors.

There exists, however, another possible explanation of her illness and its sexual undertones. Medical science, especially that of venerology, was then in its infancy. Beyond the fact that it sprang from sexual congress little was known about the origins of venereal disease and nothing at all about its cure. It was spoken of, if at all, only in whispers and hints. Elizabeth's knowledge of it must have been minimal. She would have known only that it was shameful, anti-social and degrading. She was even then something of a narcissist, worshipping at the shrine of her own face and body. The illness, its cause and probable source all combined to put a weapon into the hands of the hated court camarilla, giving them an opportunity to denigrate her and, what was no doubt worse still, to laugh at her. In her fancies she even went so far as to accuse her mother-in-law of having engineered the whole thing.

Most of Elizabeth's illnesses were psychosomatic; the symptoms described above can be self-induced. May it not have been that in her travail of mind sexual ignorance combined with sexual guilt to create a fixation on the unknown woman who was said to have supplanted her and was giving her husband the satisfaction she had failed to afford him? This along with the rumours rife at court, the whispered gossip all around her in that hot-house society, and her own terror at what was happening to her might well have combined to persuade her that he had indeed infected her. The illness and its symptoms could easily have been conjured up by her own too vivid imagination.

There seems no doubt that she did convince herself she was infected, and from that it would be but a short step to persuade him. For again there can be no doubt that, whether or not he did give her the disease, they both believed he did and that belief wrecked whatever little chance there was left of the marriage succeeding. In her torment she took the course that those of her tortured nature so often take in moments of great emotional crisis—she fled.

Queen Victoria put the Royal Yacht at her disposal. She called in it at Madeira and wintered there. She was back in the following May but in a month the symptoms recurred—which also lends support to the theory that they may have been psychosomatic—and she was off again. This time it was to Corfu whose romantic loneliness had fascinated her on her journey home.

Now there was open scepticism in the Chancelleries about the nature of her illness. 'I never heard that spot recommended by the doctors before as a summer resort for invalids suffering from complaints of the chest,' was the comment of Lord Bloomfield, the British Ambassador. Be that as it may, in Corfu she rapidly regained her health and spirits. Sea bathing, long walks and the feel of freedom completed the cure. In October the Emperor left his desk and his worries, pocketed his pride and came in person and in state to visit her in her self-imposed exile. No one knows what passed between them then. Apparently, however, she consented to return, but in her own way and in her own time. It was not until the following August that she came back to Vienna to a tumultuous welcome from the populace. Others were not quite so rapturous in their feelings about having her back. 'His expression as he helped her out of the carriage I shall never forget,' Princess Helene Taxis, her gossiping lady-in-waiting and one of the court set, wrote to a friend. 'Though her face is no longer swollen it is much thickened and changed. The fact that Prince Karl Theodor accompanied her proves how much she dreads being alone with him and all of us.'

The true fact was, of course, that she had come back on her own terms for she had won her battle. The Emperor knew that he had wronged her and knew too that he could not live without her. Henceforward he could refuse her nothing, save only for reasons of state, and not always even then.

During those two years of almost constant absence she had changed and matured. By the time of her return she had come fully to realise the power which her beauty and fascination gave her. There had been a romantic and platonic love-affair with a young and noble member of her suite. He had told her she was bewitching and it was a description many other men were to echo down the years. 'It is better not to look at her too long, for it warms one's heart far too much,' Kaiser Wilhelm of Germany told a friend. She had indeed and in full measure that power of fascination given to few women, however beautiful. But whether from repugnance, fear or an inborn shrinking from physical contact, that fascination had little that was sexual about it. It demanded submission, not satisfaction, adulation not gratification.

A contemporary demi-mondaine, Lila Buljovsky, who had hoped to ensnare Elizabeth's cousin Ludwig of Bavaria and who blamed Elizabeth for her failure, quite wrongly as it happened, wrote of her: 'She encourages gossip only because she feels such indifference towards men. It may be she mates with ghosts.'

But Bay Middleton was no ghost.

CHAPTER TWO

Bay

William George Middleton was born in 1846 into a prominent Scotch sporting family. His uncle was Master of the Fife Foxhounds for many years; his father, William Middleton, was Secretary to the Glasgow Hunt, now the Lanark and Renfrew. Besides this he had a private pack of his own which he hunted himself in Dumbartonshire. His mother was a Hamilton, an aunt of General Sir Ian Hamilton who gained fame during the South African War and later commanded the troops in the ill-fated Gallipoli expedition of 1915.

The Middletons were substantial landed proprietors but gradually their estate had to be sold off, owing to the encroachment of coal mining operated by the great coal and iron family of the Bairds. One of the less endearing members of this family was the raffish 'Abingdon' Baird who roamed London like a Regency buck out of his time and who owned Merry Hampton, the Derby winner of 1887; others became members of the Jockey Club, pillars of the Turf and Masters of Hounds. It was the sister of one of the latter, Charlotte Baird, whom Middleton was eventually to marry.

As was natural with his background, Middleton was brought up to horses and hunting. He was not, however, sent to a public school but was privately tutored at Wimbledon, possibly because his parents had a house at Prince's Gate and spent a considerable part of their time there once the hunting season was over.

He was gazetted to the 12th Lancers in 1865 and joined them at Cahir in County Tipperary. Ireland was then a sporting paradise for a young man with a thirst for life and an eye for a country. He took to it straight away and within a short time was whipping-in to the Regimental Harriers.

The Victorian sporting man had a fondness for nicknames. There was then a male cult of masculinity well summed up by Moreton Frewen, himself nicknamed 'Mortal Ruin', as 'worship of muscle and moustache.' 'Manliness' was an end in itself. These men are as remote from us now as the men of Sparta with whom, indeed, they had much in common. They set their standards and judged each other by physical bravery, 'hardness' in sporting pursuits, endurance and ability to survive and overcome danger. They were, in fact, warriors without a war. Almost all of the soldiers amongst them put the War Office under constant siege with applications for active service. But there were not enough small wars of Empire to go round and very few succeeded in their ambition to exchange the image of war which they created in their recreations for its reality in the field. Their battlefields, then, were the rolling expanses and stiff black fences of the grass countries, the broad and forbidding banks of Ireland and the mown turf of the racecourse.

Amongst this caste the use of christian names was, with very few exceptions, held in some way to imply softness or, dreaded word, effeminacy. These names were left to the women. Instead men freely bestowed sobriquets on each other and used them as a mark of affection and intimacy. 'Chicken' Hartopp, 'Doggie' Smith and 'Sugar' Candy were some of Middleton's hard-riding contemporaries. Soon his brother officers were calling him 'Bay' and by this name he became known throughout the sporting world of the British Isles and Europe. Whether it was derived from the name of the Derby winner of 1836 or from the colour of his hair which was that peculiar reddish brown that in horses is called bay, 'Bay' he remained for the rest of his life.

At the end of 1886 the regiment moved to the cavalry barracks at Ballincollig just outside Cork City. It is an indication of how successful he had been with the Regimental Harriers and how prominent he had shown himself across country that, although he was still a cornet, he was immediately made Master of the Garrison Draghounds. These he hunted for the next three seasons with such dash and fire that no one could catch him and few could live with him across the banks and ditches and the rolling country of the West Riding of the

County Cork. He began riding races too and rode his first winner at Cork Park in 1867. He was a coming man.

In appearance Bay Middleton was not particularly prepossessing. He was a shade under medium height, had nondescript if regular features, reddish sandy hair and a clipped sandy moustache. Deafness, also, had slightly affected him since boyhood. But he had about him that indefinable panache or magnetism which marks a man out from his fellows. He had, too, in superabundance—as had the Empress when she decided to use it—that most dangerous of all human qualities, charm.

He was tremendously gay, a good companion, a man who was attractive to both sexes and yet lost his popularity with neither. Outwardly he displayed almost to excess the characteristics of his class and kind, yet he was far from being completely the conventional Victorian soldier-sportsman. Had he been, he could scarcely have captured the affection of one so truly feminine as the Empress Elizabeth. Like many of those who appear to suffer from a surfeit of high spirits, in his quieter moments he was much given to melancholy. He was convinced too, rightly as it happened, that sooner or later he would come to a violent end. This other, quieter side of his nature showed in his enthusiasm for collecting Dresden china, his interest in the theatre and his ability as a whist player. He was, in fact, a suppressed eccentric and this strain in him came out in his practical joking which he carried to lengths extreme even for those days. Yet in those jokes there was something that set him apart, some flash of genius or gaiety that earned him forgiveness from almost all the victims of his wild pranks. And he had the ability to laugh if the tables were turned upon him which took the sting out of some of his more outrageous efforts.

On one occasion when staying in a country house he decided that it was not at all the thing for a member of the party to play pool after dinner in a tail coat, all the others having changed into smoking jackets. 'If you do that again tomorrow,' he warned the owner of the coat, 'I'm blessed if I don't rip it up.'

No notice was taken of the warning, for the following night the coat appeared again. As its wearer was making a stroke at the billiard table Bay, taking the coat by the tails, tore it straight up the seam. The owner did not appear in the least put out. In fact he roared with laughter. Puzzled, Middleton enquired the reason for the mirth. 'No harm done at all,' was the reply. 'This is your coat. If you go upstairs you'll find mine on my bed.' The joke had been neatly turned against the perpetrator and the first to laugh at his own expense was Middleton himself.

But the jokes with their wildness and lack of feeling do display a strain of cruelty that was latent somewhere within this complex man. He had to excel. His escapades had to be more outrageous than any one else's and nothing must stand in the way of their being so. In the 'bear-fights' that took place amongst men after dinner in smoking rooms or mess anterooms he had to emerge the victor. 'When his blood was up,' a friend recalled, 'he became almost cruel in a fight so keen was he his best friend could not expect any pity from him so long as the fight lasted.' On a horse, in the hunting field, he was superb. His great friend and hero-worshipper Charles Kinsky described him perhaps better than anyone else when he wrote: 'I don't think I ever saw a man in more perfect unison with his horse as he was. Whether they were fresh or tired he kept his horses perfectly balanced and, as a consequence, had no superior in putting a horse at a fence . . . like a good lawn tennis player who never seems to budge and to whom the ball always seems to come by itself 'Bay' to anyone following him appeared to ride straight before him, neither looking to right nor to left, while both hounds and the right places in the fences seemed always to come his way exactly where they ought to be.' But even here that strain of something different in him to set him apart came out and Kinsky commented on it: 'Bay's only fault was that he sometimes lost his temper with his horses and would then punish them very hard by hitting, spurring and jobbing them in the mouth; but, funnily enough, none of them seemed to resent this treatment afterwards though his punishments were neither necessary nor just at times.'

Therein lay his secret. No one, it appeared, not even horses, could resent him, at least for long, and very few could resist his charm. Soon the most powerful man in Ireland was to succumb to it. Since John Poyntz Spencer, fifth Earl Spencer, of Althorp Park in Northamptonshire, was to play an important, ambiguous and enigmatic part in the relationship between the Empress and Middleton, something must be said of him here.

In 1868 when Gladstone formed his first administration, he made Spencer Lord Lieutenant of Ireland at the early age of thirty-six. The office of Lord Lieutenant at that time was in a peculiar condition. Virtually its occupant enjoyed the panoply of power without either its obligations or responsibilities. Owing to the total ineffectiveness of a succession of its incumbents the office had become more a social than a political one, and the reality of power lay in the hands of the Chief Secretary.

Spencer's character was at all times difficult to fathom. Ambitious, as he was, of political preferment, he may well have resented his function being reduced to that of a gilded figurehead who presided at ceremonial occasions but did little else. If this resentment existed it was undoubtedly increased by the fact that he did not think much of the society of which he had been made the titular head. Imbued with a consciousness of his own high lineage he despised too openly the professional people, officials and rich merchants who made up most of urban Dublin society at the time and attended Castle balls and Viceregal garden parties. At first the members of this society were well-disposed towards him and christened him half-affectionately 'Rufus' from the great red beard he sported. As, however, his disdain for them grew ever more apparent and he was seen to confine his attentions and politenesses to the few great land-owners whom he considered fit to be admitted to his company, the affection turned quickly to dislike. The name was then changed to the half-contemptuous 'The Red Earl' which was to remain with him everywhere for the rest of his life. There was even talk amongst Dubliners of a boycott of his state ceremonies but this was overcome by the charm and persuasiveness of his wife. Lady Spencer's gracious nature soon won their fickle Irish hearts and caused them to forget the social slights and indignities imposed by her husband. They christened her, in turn, 'Spencer's Faerie Queen' and she became greatly loved.

Spencer's power was further diminished by the fact that he did not have a seat in the Cabinet. He found solace for his political impotence and social boredom in his passion for fox-hunting. As a boy, like many growing youths, he had been timid and frightened of hunting but this had soon disappeared and he became a bold and thrusting rider. Not at any time in his career, however, was he a polished horseman for he had a very loose seat. In Ireland he found that he was parting company with his mount rather more often than he liked. As a result he had recourse to holding on to the back of his saddle when jumping a bank. This bad and unsightly habit remained with him for the rest of his hunting days and it must have been, to say the least of it, an uncomfortable method of progression when hunting blood horses across High Leicestershire.

At the time of Spencer's entering the Viceregal Lodge the worst of the Fenian troubles were over. Ireland was, however, still unsettled. Sporadic outrages continued, though on a decreasing scale. Any person prominent in Government was to some extent exposed to personal danger. The authorities did not look kindly upon their task of giving the Lord Lieutenant protection when he went out hunting. In fact they did their best to dissuade him from going out at all.

Spencer was a strange man of many differing qualities but of his immense physical courage there was never any doubt. One of his first acts had been to borrow a hunter from the Commander of the Forces, Lord Strathnairn, and go out with the Meath. 'I inaugurated him in the hunting field', Strathnairn wrote to a friend, 'by lending him one of my best horses . . . and he was delighted with him as were the hunt. Some of the members said, "Gad, if he governs Ireland after that fashion, divil a Fenian will there be left after the hunting season!"'

Since they could not stop him hunting, the next effort of the authorities was to nominate a cavalry escort to accompany him. Watching Spencer cross the country one farmer drily commented: 'Well, if they're going to follow his Lordship I reckon they're in greater danger than he is!' Though spoken in jest the words were true and the plain fact was, of course, that the escort could not even keep him in sight. It was about this time he wrote to a friend: 'My horse fell into a blind ditch attached to a fence . . . I lost a little time in getting my horse out also my place in the first few. After going about twenty minutes . . . to my surprise up came the stag, right to me, presently three couple of hounds, then eight couple more, but no one in sight. Of course I followed this lot, and had about three miles of splendid country all to myself. When the stag was taken not a soul was to be seen, nor did a horseman appear in sight, until I had got to a road five fields off, with the hounds, not one of whom knew me. Some labourers appeared who drove them to me but when they disappeared, as they soon did, off went my reluctant followers. In about ten minutes a stray man appeared and ten minutes later the whip but not a soul besides.' Since he was also writing at the same time: 'Irish affairs are undoubtedly undergoing a crisis . . . great changes are taking place, those who are benefited are too accustomed to their old grievances to become champions of law and order and the agitators do not distinguish between real and fictitious evils,' it is apparent that the danger was real enough.

Changes were indeed taking place. The Fenians, betrayed from within, may have been defeated and suppressed but an even greater threat to English interests and power was arising. This was agrarian unrest, very soon to be skilfully channelled and exploited by Charles Stewart Parnell. Riband societies were growing, Whiteboys were active; driving and maiming of cattle was becoming commonplace. O'Donovan Rossa, in exile in America as Kossuth was in exile in England, was pursuing a policy identical with the Hungarian of exhorting his countrymen to active and violent revolt against the oppressor. The violence, too, was beginning to be more personally directed than heretofore. Landlords and their agents were threatened and in some cases shot. The Viceroy with his commanding presence and flowing red beard could scarcely be called an inconspicuous figure. No wonder the Castle authorities were worried.

Spencer himself resolutely refused to allow anyone to curtail his hunting. 'A sharp ride to covert and a good twenty minutes have kept me from collapsing. There is nothing like a good gallop across country to drive dull care away.'

Then someone hit on the idea of 'hard-riding ADCs'. Were Spencer to be provided with one or more ADCs who could at least hold their own with the Viceroy across a country, some measure of protection would be given him. There were difficulties of course in finding the right man to start the system off. In addition to their horsemanship they would have to come from a sufficiently smart regiment and have the right background to make them socially acceptable to the Viceroy and his set.

Already Bay Middleton's name as a thruster was being talked about all over sporting Ireland. Unquestionably he had all the right qualifications. The 12th Lancers were a crack regiment, he came from an old Scotch family and he crossed the country like a blaze of lightning. He was known, too, to be well able to hold his own in any sort of fight. Here was the man they were looking for.

In 1870 Bay Middleton was invited to join the Lord Lieutenant's staff as an extra ADC. He accepted with alacrity, was promoted Captain and left regimental service forever. It is said that his Colonel was not sorry to see him go since he greatly objected to Middleton's habit of blowing his hunting horn after luncheon and thus disturbing his Commanding Officer's post-prandial slumbers.

Almost immediately Middleton appears to have cast his spell over Spencer as he was to do to so many people wherever he went during his short life. First and foremost he had in supreme measure the two qualities Spencer valued above all others in a man: physical courage and the ability to ride to hounds. In addition there was the impact of his personality and the fact that he was tremendously good company, supplying for Spencer in the hunting-field and out of it the friendship and masculine companionship he had so much missed until Middleton's arrival. Soon they were inseparable and Middleton was seen to be a favourite at court. His duties were minimal; really he was a sort of fox-hunting ADC and no more, but it was quickly noticed that wherever Spencer went he went too.

At or about the same time as Middleton's arrival at the Castle, 'Chicken' Hartopp, 'the darling of the Tenth' was also appointed and for the same reasons. An enormous man of great personal fortune and a tremendous goer on horse and foot, Hartopp had the engaging habit of summoning special trains to take him all over England much as other men would hail a hansom. He, too, was in the habit of practical joking, though in his case, unlike Middleton's whose jokes were perpetrated on his social equals or superiors, they were mostly at the expense of the lower orders whom he subsequently bought off with a shower of sovereigns. Since dynamite, which he never really learned to handle, played a large part in many of these jokes, the danger to life and limb entailed was considerable and some of the payments-off came expensive. Moreton Frewen aptly described him as 'an utterly lawless sabreur'. When, a few years later, he took on the Mastership of the Kilkenny Hounds at the height of the agrarian disturbances he was accustomed to offer political opponents of the hunt his right hand to shake. If they refused or ignored it he would exclaim: 'So you'd rather have this, then,' and would brandish a clenched left fist as big as a ham in their faces. Always spoiling for a fight, he was an excellent bodyguard; but with his great weight he could not rival Middleton across a country and it was Middleton who stole the limelight and gained Spencer's special favour.

It is a tribute to Middleton's personality that despite the preference shown to him his popularity increased. His fame, too, not only across the green pastures of Meath and Kildare but as a practical joker and an unpredictable guest, spread wider afield and into all ranks of the tightly knit society of the day. From being a promising young officer he had become a social figure. Naturally such a man with the aura of success that surrounded him, his panache, his position, his high spirits and charm attracted the attention of many women, especially the predatory married women of the country house set. Bay's affairs were said to be numerous but always conducted with exemplary discretion. Towards the end of 1873, however, he embarked on a liaison with a married woman which was incandescent even by the upper-class standards of the time.

Spencer was known to be worried about the effect the affair might have on Middleton's future. When the Gladstone government fell in 1874 the Viceroy's term of office ended. He returned to Althorp and took over the Mastership of the Pytchley for the second time. Middleton sent in his papers and went with him.

His reputation had preceded him and he set about living up to it. Amongst his other qualities was a wonderful eye for a horse and he began immediately to collect a stud of blood hunters that would carry him in front across any obstacles the Shires could offer. In the course of one season his name was made. The young Duke of Portland writing years afterwards recalled 'one very good run (with the Meynell) in Lord Waterpark's time when we ran right into the high ground in Derbyshire, jumping two or three stone walls at the end. I remember it well, not only as being a good run but because it was the first time I ever met Bay Middleton out hunting. I can see him now. He was riding a thick-set grey hunter and he went first all the way.'

Hunting diaries of the day are full of him and his exploits: of his jumping a fence no one else would take on and being alone with hounds; of his jumping over the hunted fox lying in a ditch. 'Bay had the best of it,' the expression appears again and again in all the recollections of the period. 'A prominent member of the noble army of "bruisers" who sees no good in fighting or hunting unless it is carried on at fever-heat. He owns a stud that is second to none and is sure to see the cream of any good thing,' is a typical entry.

He was a welcome guest at great houses: the doors of Althorp were always open to him; he was elected a member of I Zingari, that exclusive band of wandering cricketers, and began to be known, too, as a man about town. Portland put him down amongst the smartest of the sporting dandies, along with 'Doggie' Smith (his great rival across Leicestershire and the Shires) and George Lambton. 'They were all', Portland wrote, 'men of good and manly figure which set off their well-fitting and perfectly chosen clothes.'

In February each year he was accustomed to go to Scotland for a few weeks' hunting with the Eglinton. There he met and courted Charlotte Baird, a member, as has been said, of the mining family whose interests had encroached upon the Middleton estates. In 1875 they became engaged to be married. The future looked to be the conventional one of the well-to-do fox-hunting and racing man of the time. But it did not turn out quite that way.

CHAPTER THREE

A Taste of Freedom

During the years following her return from Corfu the Empress slowly but surely consolidated her independence. More and more she turned away from the cold and hostile Viennese towards Hungary and the Hungarians. Here she found a society very different from that which she detested in Vienna. The nobles were gay, dashing, uninhibited—and horse lovers. There were four Crown stud farms of which Kisber and Mezoheyges were the most important; there were racecourses at Pardubitz in Bohemia, where both flat racing and steeplechasing took place and at Alag, the Hungarian Newmarket. In Hungary at that time, too, there was a floating population of Englishmen, soldiers, gentlemen riders, noblemen, grooms and adventurers. They came out to buy troopers or thoroughbreds or to sell them, for the authorities at Kisber were constantly importing English blood, to ride races, make love, gamble and cut a dash. Sporting Hungarians and sporting Englishmen had much in common. They liked blood horses, big fences, high play and smart, sophisticated married women. Amongst the great families it was the exception rather than the rule not to have an English stud groom or master of horse.

As well as racing there was stag- and fox-hunting run on English lines. It has often been said that Elizabeth introduced these to Hungary. This is not so though she did much to develop them. Racing and hunting on English lines had been introduced to Hungary in the eighteen-thirties by Count Istvan Syechingi, a statesman, reformer and Anglophile. By the fifties there were several private packs of foxhounds. The great family of Esterhazy had one, Count Kolzyi another with hounds and hunt staff specially imported from England; and Prince Ferdinand Kinsky, the head of that mighty house, hunted a pack of harriers over his own vast estates in Bohemia, as did the Larisch family at Solza.

Though she did not at first take part in these pursuits Elizabeth explored the country on horseback, often accompanied only by the faithful Holmes. The loneliness and solitude of the great plains appealed to her solitary and romantic nature. The wild horses that thronged them entranced her. 'How I should like to spend my life on these Hungarian plains—just tending to these splendid creatures,' she wrote to a friend with, it must be said, typical hyperbole. Franz Joseph now made no attempt to interfere. Indeed soon, within their marriage and in social matters, it was she who was dictating to him.

It was the education of the Crown Prince which brought about the clash that confirmed forever her right to pursue her own wayward paths as she wished and as her tastes dictated.

The Crown Prince had been subjected to an even more disastrous upbringing than that of the Prince of Wales in England. Gondrecourt, to whose care Franz Joseph had consigned him with instructions to make a man of him, was a sadist. After one particularly disgraceful incident designed to 'test his courage' had been brought to her attention Elizabeth, never as a rule particularly interested in her children's upbringing or well-being, seized the opportunity to issue an ultimatum. 'It must be either Gondrecourt or myself . . . I further desire that everything concerning my own personal affairs, such, for instance, as the choice of those about my person, my place of residence, all changes in domestic arrangements, should be left for me alone to decide.' The Emperor capitulated.

This state of affairs did not pass unobserved either in Vienna or Budapest. Though the bulk of the Austrian Court families still disliked and resented her and made little attempt to conceal these feelings, the more astute among them came quickly to realise that in her, now, a new power had arisen and, furthermore, that the influence of the Archduchess was waning. The first of those to recognise that she was no longer a nonentity but someone to be cultivated and courted was the Kinsky family.

The Kinskys were the grandest and most powerful of all the ruling few in Vienna. Countess Rosa Kinsky had been a close friend of the Emperor Joseph II. Her son married Marie Liechtenstein, thus uniting two great houses. Princess Marie, an immensely able and ambitious woman, saw to it that her brother Rudolph Liechtenstein secured the position of Chief Lord High Steward which gave him almost unlimited power over the household. Between them they distributed patronage and influence on a princely scale. They had no intention of being ousted or deprived of these privileges by the growing social power of the Empress. In addition to their rank and standing the men of the Kinsky family had the immense advantage in the Empress's eyes of possessing striking good looks and being fine horsemen. Soon they had won her admiration and confidence. Ferdinand Kinsky was made First Equerry of the Royal Stud and a nephew, Count Bellegarde, promoted to the sinecure but influential position of Chief Master of the Imperial Kitchens. Further favours followed. Shortly after these appointments a malicious jingle, written by someone outside the chosen circle who had failed to obtain preferment, began to circulate in society drawing rooms. It had as its refrain:

> I beg your pardon one and all,
> Alas, I'm not from Kinsky Hall.

In Budapest, too, one man sized up the situation immediately and resolved to make his country profit from the Empress's increasing influence on her husband. Count Julius Andrassy had parted from Kossuth and his doctrine of violence. He had left England to serve out his exile in Paris and had let it be known that he was now committed to compromise and constitutional reform. In 1857 he was pardoned, his estates were restored to him and he returned to Hungary. An immensely attractive man, a patriot, a pragmatist and a schemer, he too soon won his way into the Empress's trust and confidence. It was through him that, after she had gained her freedom to make her own appointments, it was two Hungarians who filled the positions of her chief ladies-in-waiting. These were Ida Ferenczy and Countess Festetics. In return it was through her that his and his country's steady advancement to power and freedom was begun and maintained. He was more than half in love with her throughout his long life, and she was certainly charmed by his attentions and attracted by his gallantry.

He was the sort of man she liked—a cavalier, a gay and dashing figure who sat a horse like a centaur. Amorist though he was with her, he appears to have suppressed his sexual inclinations in favour of his political ambitions. But he was always at her side, accompanying her to race meetings at Alag and Pardubitz and riding with her unescorted through the lonely woods.

Sometimes she rode alone in these woods. There were then roaming them packs of savage dogs that had been known to attack and pull down horses and their riders. Fearful for her safety he had made for her a tiny, beautifully wrought lady's revolver, chased and damascened and inlaid in gold. On the barrel he had engraved his name and the southern European sign against the evil eye. A leather holster belt specially measured to fit her tiny waist was made to carry the weapon which he then presented to her with the request that she wear it always when she rode alone so as to relieve the concern her friends felt for her. Until the woods were finally cleared of their savage inhabitants she did so and the little revolver was her constant companion on all her rides.

Ida Ferenczy had been briefed to keep him informed of all that went on in the household and it was she who told him that on one of her expeditions the Empress had seen and fallen in love with an abandoned estate at Gödollo some eighteen miles from Budapest. Not only that but she was writing to the Emperor about it with a view to acquiring it.

On receiving her letter the Emperor, for once, had to sound a warning note. 'Do not look over it as though we wanted to buy it', he wrote, 'for I have no money at present and we shall have to economise enormously in these hard times . . . Nearly half the stables will have to be sold and we shall have to live very simply.' The letter was genuine enough since, enormously rich though he was, there was then a financial crisis in Austria and he was trying to cut back household expenditure. Its tone shows that he had learnt, at last and too late, not to dictate to her but, like his mother, he could never bring himself to treat Hungarians with anything other than distrust and he must have dreaded her increasing commitment to his other kingdom. It was in any event too late to alter his tactics towards her.

Andrassy learnt of his reply from Ferenczy almost as soon as it arrived and stored the information away for future use. When the *Ausgleich*, the joining of the monarchies, took place in 1867 he asked if the Emperor and Empress would graciously accept from the Hungarian nation the house and lands of Gödollo as their residence in Hungary. The response was an immediate and enthusiastic acceptance, especially on her part. 'It was an enormous pleasure to me', she wrote to Franz Joseph, 'to hear that Gödollo is to be our property.'

Now she had a house of her own in a land she loved. Here at last she felt she had an opportunity of being herself, of creating her own circle away from prying and disapproving eyes, of living her own life the way she wished. She would have about her at Gödollo only those she had chosen herself, not from reasons of rank or birth but because she liked them and because they had similar tastes to her own. Gödollo was admirably suited to her purposes and it had all the romantic and historical associations which she loved. Although it was in decay when she received it, the Dukes of Grassakiovic had in their time bred Hungary's finest horses there and one of them had erected a statue to his favourite charger in its park. Its moors and forests covered over thirty thousand acres; its vast stretches of *putsa* gave wonderful gallops for her horses; its lakes and marshes provided snipe shooting for the Emperor and Rudolph whenever they cared to visit.

Rudolph, in fact, was not turning out the way either of his parents wanted. In him the Wittelsbach genes, always erratic and eccentric, combined to produce a nervous over-sensitive child, lacking both confidence and mental balance. Gondrecourt's savage tuition had killed the few weak strains of Habsburg sturdiness that ran in him and had turned him into a pleasure-seeking and self-pitying neurotic. Shooting was the only sport he cared for and even there he appeared to take an unhealthy and almost sadistic delight in the killing of wild and beautiful things. Worse still from the point of view of both his parents, who were at least united in demanding that any man about them should display courage and equestrian ability (Franz Joseph was said at this time to choose his generals by the way they sat a horse and, judging by their failures in the field, he might as well have done), he was a useless and frightened horseman. He parted from the saddle with extreme ease and had no mastery or control of his mount. Soon he made it clear to his parents that he did not like hitting the ground and hated horses.

Franz Joseph was furious. After all he had conquered his own fears and his lack of inborn ability. 'Every rider must have a fall now and then and get practice in falling,' he wrote to Rudolph. This cold comfort did not serve to inspire his son to any greater efforts. In fact, as has happened to other nervous youths, his parents' over-keenness frightened him off altogether. Soon he abandoned riding except when required of him on ceremonial occasions and mounted a horse with extreme reluctance even then. All this did not make him a very welcome guest at Gödollo where Elizabeth had encouraged a group of gentlemen to start a pack of hounds.

But there were others who were. Andrassy assiduously pursued the fox; the Kinskys came for the hunting as did Prince Rudi Liechtenstein. The British Ambassador, Sir Andrew Buchanan, was favoured with an invitation; even the Emperor occasionally put in an appearance. Prince 'Nicky' Esterhazy, though a member of the family who had provided her with her first and hated lady-in-waiting, was forgiven because of his horsemanship and knowledge of the chase. He was made MFH and had the run of the Palace and its stables. In those stables were twenty-six English-bred hunters under the charge of Holmes, kept for her own use and those of her selected friends.

One thing she disliked about her Hungarian hunting was that if the meet were outside the confines of the Gödollo demesne crowds came to stare at her. Always she had demanded privacy and shunned the public eye. As we have seen, on the eve of her wedding she had expressed her distaste for being stared at 'like a freak in a circus'. This distaste was more acute now and the fact that the people crowded about her from love and admiration did nothing to lessen it. 'They express this feeling', wrote Andrassy, 'by following her too closely . . . and no one can prevent this.' She was also probably the first Royalty to suffer the attentions of surreptitious photographers anxious to record and exploit for left-wing Austrian newspapers their Empress's going-on in the sister kingdom, and they made her furious.

To deter these public stares and over-eager cameramen she had made for her a small leather fan. This was hung at her saddle-bow as another woman might carry a pair of spare gloves. At meets or checks she would open this fan and hold it in front of her face. It was a practice which was to produce some mockery and derision from her own sex in England later on. They did not understand, or affected not to, that it was not used for any cosmetic purpose but solely to avoid publicity.

Gödollo gave her a sort of happiness. She rode 'devilish well'. She could hold her own with any man in the hunt. 'It was a very fine run,' she wrote to the Emperor after one of these. 'Holmes and I led the field. But the fox ran to earth.' That was one of the troubles: the fox too often ran to earth for, owing to the sandy terrain, it was almost impossible to stop the country adequately. The woods and forests, too, ensured that foxes seldom ran straight or far. Also, the season was very short. It began after the harvest was gathered in, usually early in September, and ended on St Hubert's Day (3 November). There was very little jumping and what there was consisted almost entirely of small open ditches. Her restless and aspiring nature told her that this, good though it was, was not the real thing.

The Prince of Wales had visited the Vienna Exhibition of 1873. He had dined with her and, knowing her tastes, had talked of horses and hunting with her. The Prince was then still in his thirties. Increasing corpulence and indulgence in the pleasures of the flesh had not yet brought about his abandonment of the chase. He still on occasions hunted in the Shires. Moreover he went most gallantly to hounds, moving a countryman on one occasion, mistaking him for his equerry, to inform him he had better take more care of his royal master, 'for if you don't that young bugger will break his neck!'

During dinner he had elaborated on the delights and excitements he had enjoyed out hunting. Almost certainly he was, in his amiable way, only making conversation, talking to his hostess about what he thought would interest her most. He can scarcely have realised the flame he was lighting or the train of events he was starting off. She listened attentively and then and there was born in her the ambition to hunt in England and the determination to fulfil that ambition at all costs.

Her younger sister Marie, the Queen of Naples, also furthered her eagerness to taste the thrill of English fox-hunting. The throne of Naples had been lost in the revolution of 1861 and she was now, to use her own expression, 'a Queen on the retired list'. Elizabeth envied her her freedom and listened, rapt, to her stories.

The Queen had rented a hunting box near Althorp and had become friendly with Spencer. She appears to have met Middleton at Althorp or to have seen him out hunting and admired the way he went. It seems all but certain that she must have mentioned his name to her sister when telling her of the runs they had had and the fences they had jumped. Bay Middleton, 'the bravest of the brave', was a name which invariably came up whenever hunting people talked together during those years. It is not unreasonable to suppose that the Empress, fired with a desire to hunt in the Shires, also wished to meet the man she heard of as the best and bravest across that formidable country. In 1874 she saw it for the first time but she did not then meet Bay Middleton.

The Queen of Naples continued her insistence that the Empress should visit England and in the summer of 1874 she decided to go. Always to some extent she had to camouflage these foreign tours since they were profoundly disapproved of by both the Austrian authorities and the court. Franz Joseph had to some degree to be wooed for although she had won her independence there was always the possibility that he might find financial or other reasons for putting a stop to them. The excuse this time was that her daughter, Valerie, required the sea-bathing that the Isle of Wight alone could provide. She travelled incognito under her favourite alternative title, the Countess of Hohenembs, and arrived on 2nd August 1874. Countess Festetics and Ida Ferenczy were in the suite. Almost immediately Queen Victoria drove over from Osborne to visit her. The Queen was struck by the Empress's beauty and recorded her in her diary as 'looking very lovely, like a beautiful picture with her magnificent hair in which there is a rich tint of auburn braided all round her head and forming as it were a diadem. Her waist is smaller than anything one can imagine and her walk most graceful.'

The Queen, too, may well have felt some slight stirrings of envy at the Empress's radiant beauty and slim figure. She had once in her youth fancied herself on a horse, had dressed in the smartest black and green velvet habits and had had herself painted on horseback by Landseer and others. The sight of the Empress may have reminded her that she had once, as Lady Longford says, consoled herself for her lack of beauty by the fact that she looked superb on a horse. It was no longer true but the memory may have lingered.

As for the Empress, once she felt out of sympathy with a person it followed that she would avoid his or her company in the future if she could. As always her personal feelings overcame the role she should have played. Indiscretions, and sometimes antipathy, resulted. This is what happened now. She refused two invitations to dinner at Osborne and Queen Victoria was not pleased. 'I did so', the Empress wrote to her mother, with a naïveté which was engaging if it was nothing else, 'because that sort of thing bores me.'

In fact, that summer, she was quite determined to be a private person and to enjoy herself amongst those whom she found interesting or entertaining. From what she had seen of Queen Victoria's entourage it seemed almost as stuffy as Franz Joseph's and she wanted nothing to do with it. Instead it was her intention to have some fun with horses and she was not long in finding it.

First she went to London to look at what horseflesh was on offer and to ride in the Row with the Ambassador, Count Beust. Since the season was over and Society out of Town she was left much to her own devices which was what she wanted. The prices she was asked for the horses she saw proving too high, she moved on to Melton to look for hunters. There again, mindful for once of the Emperor's pocket, she did not buy. After that she went to Belvoir Castle as the guest of the Duke of Rutland.

She had her first sight of English hounds on 24 August 1874. It was only cub-hunting and they did not do much but she was excited at the feel of an English hunter underneath her and the thud of his hooves on English grass. The Queen of Naples introduced her to Lord Spencer who had come over from Althorp. Spencer was captivated immediately and both of them implored her to return when the season proper had got really under way.

Also out were the Baltazzi brothers, Hector and Alexander, Levantines with Hungarian connections, brilliant horsemen both of them. Educated at Rugby, they had stud farms and estates in England, Austria and Hungary. Their sister Baroness Vetsera was quietly pushing her way into Viennese society. The brothers, too, were socially ambitious. The Queen of Naples, who always had her eye on money and the main chance, was prepared to do everything to help them. Good-looking and dashing, they quickly caught the eye of the Empress and she had them presented to her. 'Great caution is necessary,' wrote Marie Festetics in her diary after observing this. 'The brothers are devoted to sport, ride splendidly and push themselves in everywhere; but they are dangerous to us, for they are quite English, and on account of the horses!'

Hardly was the Empress back in the Isle of Wight than she was again in the midst of horses and their riders. The Castle Club on the Island, hearing of her trip to the Shires, decided to put on a race meeting for her. Arthur Yates, one of the leading gentlemen riders of the day, was given the task of organising it. When the Empress was informed of their intention she clapped her hands with delight and immediately sent off to Hancock, the London jeweller, to design a cup for the winner of the principal race.

When the day came round the Queen of Naples and her husband joined the Empress in her carriage. They had brought with them Hector Baltazzi who had secured a ride. There were three contests: the Imperial Cup, a Consolation Race and a Scratch Race. Mr Weeks, an Isle of Wight farmer, won the cup. The only faller was Charnwood carrying the Empress's own Austrian colours of black and orange as a compliment to her. Hector Baltazzi won the Scratch Race.

The Empress presented the 'massive silver-gilt two-handled loving cup' to Mr Weeks. There was tremendous cheering; Mr Weeks filled the cup with champagne. It was passed around to the toast of 'Health and long life to the Empress of Austria!' More cheers rent the heavens. Champagne flowed like water. What Queen Victoria, a few miles away in seclusion at Osborne, thought of it all was not recorded.

These blissful few weeks were crowned with joy when Lady Dudley, who had seen her out cubbing and admired her, presented her with a bloodlike English hunter. She sailed from England more determined than ever to return.

CHAPTER FOUR

The Meeting

The promised return had, however, to be postponed since affairs of state intervened. But, once the Empress's mind was really set on an objective, she usually attained it. While quietly preparing the way for a second visit she filled in the time hunting from Gödollo and taking lessons from Elie Renz, the daughter of the ringmaster, in training horses for circus-riding with, more often than not, herself on their backs. A new groom, Allen, had been sent out from England by the Queen of Naples to replace Holmes who was getting on in years. With Allen she rode in the Prater and schooled Lady Dudley's English hunter over the steeplechase fences on the Freudenau, the Vienna racecourse. She had had a glimpse of the big English fences that day from Belvoir and was intelligent enough to realise that they would take considerably more riding over than anything she had so far faced. Hence her desire to get the feel of a big horse jumping fast and big and out of his stride. The only place she could get this in Vienna was the racecourse. It need hardly be said that the spectacle of the Empress and her groom jumping fences together in public, or practically in public, was held at court to be unedifying to say the least. Feeling against her, too, was just beginning to spread to the general public. They had been willing to take her to their hearts for her beauty and her bravery. Now her open disregard for their admiration, her expressed preference for Hungary and the Hungarians shown by her long absences from the capital and her choice of members of the other monarchy for her personal suite, combined to diminish her popularity. Nor did they approve any more than the court did of her informal habits and her choice of grooms for escorts.

As usual with her, too, once she had become fascinated by a pursuit or some aspect of it, she carried that fascination to extremes. She developed a veritable passion for jumping her horses and this nearly led to disaster. It was one thing to school over the properly made fences of a steeplechase course but quite another when she instructed Allen to erect temporary obstacles in the park of a château in France where she was visiting.

The Countess Festetics, who was a profoundly possessive and jealous woman, believed that Allen consistently over-faced and over-horsed her mistress. Elizabeth would have none of this. She told the Countess that Allen was, if possible, an even more perfect gentleman than Holmes. With Allen's active encouragement she insisted on having a go over the fences in the park with a horse which had been sent to her to try. The horse came down and the Empress came off. It was high summer and the ground was hard. She lost her hat, hit her head and received slight concussion.

The household panicked. The Emperor was telegraphed; he wanted to dash to her bedside, thereby causing confusion in the chancelleries, for relations with France were strained at the time and her visit was strictly incognito. When he was restrained by his advisers he wrote her anguished letters telling her, amongst other things, that the whole world was talking about her.

The only person to remain calm in all this fuss was the victim of the accident and her own whims: Elizabeth herself. 'I am grieved at giving you such a fright', she wrote to the Emperor in words strangely reminiscent of his own letter to Rudolph, 'but you and I are really prepared for such accidents . . . I shall be very glad to have more horses again at Gödollo. I had too few here to work properly and I am anxious to show that I have not lost my nerve on account of this fall . . .'

By the end of the month she had her wish for she was back at Gödollo and, despite the Emperor's cautions and protests, hunting again with all her old dash. She was, however, finding it increasingly boring and wearisome, not the real thing at all, and she now resolved that nothing would prevent her from returning to England and experiencing the hunting there herself.

Early next year, 1896, at the age of thirty-eight, she managed it. There was just then nothing of state importance to prevent her travelling. As usual the Emperor capitulated and gave way to her wishes. He made only one rather pathetic stipulation and that was that her doctor, Langyi, should accompany her always when she was hunting. A carriage was to be placed at his disposal and he was instructed to drive around for as long as she was out so as to be at hand in case of an accident. It was agreed, too, that Bayzand, the stud-groom, should act as 'rider in attendance' and hunt with her at all times so that he would be present in the field to help should mishap befall.

The Queen of Naples was, that season, hunting in the Grafton country. Correspondence passed between her and Linger, the Empress's secretary, about the renting of a suitable house for the Imperial visit. The choice fell on Easton Neston, the Hawksmoor house near Towcester, formerly the seat of the Earls of Pomfret.

The Empress travelled as Countess Hohenembs and insisted that the visit was to be in no way considered a formal one. But she brought with her a sizeable suite including Baron Nopcsa, the Master of her Household, Countess Festetics as lady-in-waiting, Langyi, her doctor, Frau von Feyfalik, her hairdresser and 'dresser' in chief, together with Bayzand, stud-groom and 'rider in attendance' and Allen. In addition her immediate friends and admirers Rudi Liechtenstein, Counts Hans and Heinrich Larisch and Prince Ferdinand Kinsky came along for the hunting and the fun.

These latter were swells of some magnitude indeed. Liechtenstein, in addition to his position as Chief Lord High Steward which made him in effect master of the court, was about to be made Master of the Imperial Horse. He held therefore the two greatest appointments in the Emperor's gift. Steadfast, loyal, a magnificent-looking man who owned vast estates in Moravia, he wielded greater influence at court than anyone save the Emperor himself. As well as gaining and keeping the trust and confidence of the Empress, he and Albert of Saxony were the closest, indeed perhaps the only, real male friends of the Emperor. He trusted them implicitly and it was said that with them alone he would sometimes drop for once the cloak of reserve with which he surrounded himself.

The Larischs were the sons of Johann Larisch who was

Marshal of the Court, another position of high importance and consequence. They themselves were Court Chamberlains, a lesser honour but still one that was coveted. The Larisch family owned great estates at Solza in Silesia where, as has been said, Johann kept his own pack of harriers. In addition, he was Master of the Pardubitz Staghounds for a few years before being succeeded by his son Heinrich. They, too, were close to the Emperor as well as being of the Empress's inner circle. The Mastership of the Pardubitz was the Emperor's appointment. The pack had been formed by a committee on a sort of co-operative basis, each member owning shares. The Emperor held the controlling interest. By virtue of this he insisted that the officers of the local garrison should have the right to hunt without paying a subscription or without waiting for an invitation from the committee. He also personally scrutinised all damage claims and insisted on liberal settlements. The Mastership was therefore only given to someone upon whom he knew he could rely and was granted and approved almost as an Imperial honour.

Prince Ferdinand Kinsky was, of course, the head of that great and powerful family who have already been mentioned and who were allied by marriage to the Liechtensteins.

The departure of the Empress did not pass without incident for the whole enterprise presented itself to Viennese society as both eccentric and outrageous. 'People in Society', the British Ambassador Buchanan reported, 'are disposed to censure her proceedings generally . . .' But it was not only members of Society who disapproved of this expedition, for ordinary folk, too, were astonished and horrified when they heard of it. To such an extent did their feelings run that it was proposed to hold a demonstration at the railway station to protest against her departure. The secret police learned of this plot only just in time to alert the uniformed branch. They broke up the gathering almost before it had formed and the Empress left full of joyful anticipation and quite unaware of any unseemliness.

She did, however, succeed in having a minor spar with Queen Victoria on her arrival in England. When passing through London, being smitten with a sudden desire to obey the proprieties, she expressed a wish to pay her respects to the

Queen. That lady, however, had neither forgotten nor overlooked the incidents of the year before and the Empress received the curt reply that Her Majesty was too busy to receive her. 'Imagine if I were so ill-bred!' she dashed off in a hasty note to Franz Joseph, quite overlooking her own earlier behaviour. It was always her way to forget what she did to others and remember every detail of what they did to her.

Royal occasions were to her only minor matters just then. Sport was the thing, after all, which she had come for. She arrived at Towcester station by the mid-day train on 6 March looking radiant, and drove to Easton Neston to the accompaniment of a welcoming peal of bells from the local church.

The following day, Monday, she hunted with the Grafton and on Tuesday, at Lord Spencer's invitation, she drove over to Althorp for luncheon.

The Grafton country though big and strongly fenced is not one of the true galloping countries for it rides very heavy. But the Pytchley, where Althorp was situated and of which Spencer was the Master, is a flyer's paradise. The Empress wanted to gallop and jump and to do both at full stretch. Nothing else would satisfy her. She conveyed her excitement and enthusiasm to Spencer who once more fell completely under her spell. One can hardly blame him. When she was enjoying herself her lovely face lit up and her amber eyes gleamed and flashed. Edward VII remembered her as 'full of fire', after enjoying her company on one of these occasions. When happy she would bewitch anyone.

Spencer arranged to bring out his hounds on a bye-day for her special pleasure the following morning. Then he came to realise that he faced the problem of providing her with a pilot. He had seen her cub-hunting with the Belvoir the year before and knew that she could ride. His informants from the Grafton country would almost certainly have told him of the events of the day before. Frank Beers, the huntsman, had been delighted with her and the way she had crossed a big country in front in a fast run. 'A very pretty run,' he had noted in his diary that night. 'The Empress rode beautifully.' And he had presented her with the brush. She was, in fact, and by now Spencer must have learned it, as good as she looked.

In Spencer's estimation the honour of piloting her could only be adequately accepted and fulfilled by one man and that was Bay Middleton. The embers of the incandescent love affair with the married woman were still flickering. With this in mind he wondered if it would, however, be quite proper to place the Empress in Middleton's care. Had he known her as well then as he was to do later he would have realised that the Empress cared little for convention, either in the hunting field or off it. At all events he appears to have rapidly overcome whatever scruples in the matter that he had, for he went to Middleton and asked him if he would pilot the Empress the next day.

The response he received was scarcely encouraging. Middleton had not then met the lady and knew very little of her save that she was some foreign royalty who presumably imagined she could ride. He must have had visions of hanging about waiting for gaps, taking a line of gates or, worse still, riding the road. He was always very conscious of his own reputation and his first reaction was flatly to refuse the offered privilege. 'What is an empress to me?' he said. 'She'll only hold me back. You know very well I must ride my own line.' When Spencer reassured him that he need not be in any way apprehensive about her abilities he at length relented and agreed to do it 'just this once'.

Some remarks are too good not to be repeated. Besides, Bay was a character and what he said was almost always passed on whether it was worth it or not, and in this case it certainly was. Whether Spencer himself related it or whether someone heard the exchange and told of it cannot now be known but, from whatever source it came, the remark was very soon all over the place and before nightfall it had reached the ears of the Empress. The Queen of Naples, who was said herself to have had an eye for Bay and who was never in any event averse from making mischief, may have been responsible for this. It had one immediate and not altogether surprising effect: it put the Empress on her mettle.

The following morning her toilette was prepared with especial care. 'Her facial preparation was made up of cold cream camphor and borax. There was also a strawberry ointment made from the juice of wild berries mixed with vaseline and preserved with salicylic acid.'

The fact that she never wore a petticoat caused some scandal amongst Victorian matrons when they heard of it. Instead she had had made for her a special garment of the finest chamois into which she was sewn and which she wore next to her skin. Her habits were stretched and moulded to her figure and it often took hours before she was fully satisfied with their fit on a hunting morning. That day, we are told, she wore a blue habit with gold buttons.

When at last she was ready she was driven over to Althorp. The meet was timed for one o'clock and Spencer had done his best to keep it private. His efforts met with little success, for a huge throng had turned out to meet the Empress. The news that she had performed well with the Grafton and that Bay Middleton was to pilot her had heightened everyone's interest. Some came to admire, some to stare and some—mostly her own sex—unquestionably to sneer.

To appreciate fully the interest and excitement that her arrival aroused it is necessary to understand what she was taking on and how formidable was the task which she was setting herself. Those were the great, some would say the greatest, days of English fox-hunting. There was then little or no wire; there were no tarmac roads and no motor-cars to break up the country and prevent hounds running far, fast and straight. Above all there was no plough: every inch of land was pasture, good galloping English grass which stock had grazed for centuries. The Pytchley grass, it was said, 'would fatten an ox to the acre' and of all the grass countries it was probably the most strongly fenced to control this stock. A feature of the country was the Pytchley 'oxer' specially designed to contain these big cattle. This consisted of a stout timber rail erected a few feet out from the cut-and-laid or stake-and-bound fence to keep the stock away from it. The rail imposed on a horse meeting it the task of standing right back and reaching out for the fence beyond it. If there was a rail on either side, thus constituting a 'double-oxer', the obstacle was a formidable one indeed. A few of these fences were literally unjumpable and until the turn of the century the Pytchley hunt servants carried small axes to deal with these in the same way that hunt servants now often carry wire-cutters.

In addition to the oxers there were the 'Pytchley bottoms' which the historian of the hunt describes thus: 'A bottom is a gully cut in the deep soil at the bottom of a watershed. They vary in depth from two to ten feet, or even more, and are anything from six to thirty feet wide. As they are protected by a very strong bullfinch they are unjumpable in many places.' (A 'bullfinch' is a fence so high it cannot be jumped and has to be brushed through.)

Hounds in the flying countries were bred for speed—they had to be—and hunts were ridden at a tremendous pace. In those days the speed of a good hunt was often quite as fast as a steeplechase over the semi-natural courses of the day and faster than that of many point-to-points. The horses themselves, bred from the best for the best, could and often did contest steeplechases if their owners were so inclined. A fall from one of those big, blood hunters stretching himself over an oxer or misjudging a sudden drop had all the impact and risk of a fall in a race. This risk was increased in the case of a woman, hampered as she was by the voluminous habits of the time. If the horse fell these habits often ensnared their wearers in the crippling pummels of the side-saddles in which they rode. It took nerve of a high order for anyone, man or woman, but especially woman, to ride in front when the Pytchley hounds were running hard on a burning scent in those great days of fox-hunting in the seventies.

'Don't worry, mark my words, they'll come back,' Goodall, the huntsman, used to say when he saw a newcomer cutting a dash across the Pytchley country. He was in some position to know since he hunted the country for twenty-two years. During most of those years Lord Spencer was Master. For some reason best known to himself he mounted Goodall indifferently, to the ultimate ruin of the huntsman's once unshakable nerve.

When the news spread abroad that this lovely foreigner, an empress to boot, was about to try to cross the country behind none other than Bay Middleton and that Bay had sworn not to spare her, the whole fashionable fox-hunting world was set agog.

Bayzand had brought the horses over. Rudi Liechtenstein, her 'handsome prince', and Heinrich Larisch accompanied her to the meet. In the great hall at Althorp Bay Middleton was brought up by Spencer and presented to her.

Although it was a bye-day the gentlemen wore scarlet in

honour of the Empress. There is no doubt that Bay, too, together with his valet, had taken pains with his dress for he was conscious of his clothes, and he was turned out to perfection. The tail coat, cut like an evening coat, had been introduced to the hunting field by Captain Owen Williams, a leading member of the Marlborough House set, some ten yearrs earlier but very few of the top-sawyers had as yet adopted it. Middleton wore a scarlet coat high-buttoned and cut away like a morning-coat, white leather breeches, boots a little lower on the leg than is customary today, with flesh-pink tops, garter straps that tied and did not buckle and spurs long in the shank with wicked rowels. Like the other men about him, from his slicked-down hair to the heels of his boned and polished boots he gleamed as he moved. And there were, approximately, three hundred of them, all valetted to the last inch and the last instant before their appearance. The colour and glory of a Shire field in those days was indeed something to be marvelled at.

She was, or so it is said, cold enough when she greeted him. She may well, indeed, have wondered what it was that had made this stocky, rather ordinary-looking man of thirty already a living legend in the hunting field and out of it. He, for his part, never unappreciative of female beauty, must have been struck immediately by her loveliness.

Most of the pictures of Elizabeth quite fail to capture or do justice to the surpassing grace and beauty to which everyone who came in contact with her bore testimony. Winterhalter's court pictures, possibly because he tried too hard to record the strange quality of elusiveness that haunted her expression, are failures and most of the photographs are empty and lifeless. Fortunately there is one picture which is a total success and has recorded her almost exactly as Middleton must have seen her that day. It is by the unknown artist C.de Grimm and was done as an illustration for *Vanity Fair*, the Society paper.

De Grimm has painted her in her riding habit against the fanciful background of a timber stile upon which she sits. A tall hat is perched at a rakish angle on her lovely hair and a long cutting whip is between her slim fingers. She is looking out over the rolling green fields of the country she came to know so well and cross so wonderfully. Despite the severe cut of the habit and the voluminous folds of its skirt she is the ultimate in feminity.

One has only to glance at the picture to realise the fascination she must have had for Middleton and all the others whom in those galloping years she conquered with her grace and charm.

Middleton, however, was far from conquered then. Spencer had, after all, landed him in a terribly difficult position. He, too, had his detractors and his enemies as anyone has who puts himself out in front, away from the ruck. And not all those upon whom the practical jokes had been played were prepared to suffer them gladly.

Leslie Ward, the Society artist who was 'Spy' of *Vanity Fair*, had the previous year attended a dance at Oakleigh Court, the home of Lord Otho Paget. Middleton and the Prince Imperial, the son of the Empress Eugenie, were also among the guests. Paget was inordinately proud of his membership of the Royal Yacht Squadron and its burgee invariably flew from the flagstaff of his stately home. Middleton, with the Prince Imperial as his accomplice, during the evening climbed the tower where the flagstaff was and substituted a towel for the RYS burgee. The next morning the whole houseparty saw an ordinary bedroom towel flying in the breeze instead of the proud badge of social exclusiveness. 'The Prince Imperial thought this was a great joke', commented Ward, 'but I never heard that the owner shared his opinion.' A few months before that when in Ireland with an IZ team, Middleton had incurred the cold fury of Sir Chandos Leigh, the eminent Parliamentary barrister, brother of Lord Leigh and Captain of the team. They had all been entertained to dinner at Dublin Castle by the Duke of Abercorn, who had succeeded Spencer as Lord Lieutenant. After the meal Leigh presented the freedom of I Zingari to the Duchess. In order to do so he had to go down on his bended knee and make a short speech. As he was in that position Middleton came up behind and tied his coat-tails in such a way as to make it all but impossible for him to rise again without falling over. The company could not contain their laughter at the predicament into which the unfortunate Leigh had been put. Since he had his back to them Leigh could not, of course, ascertain the reason for the gales of laughter coming from behind him. He soon did so, however, when he tried to rise. It took him some time to forget the incident and what he conceived to be the humiliation he had suffered at Middleton's hands.

Then, too, Bay's fame as a thruster had brought its usual concomitant of jealousy in its wake. If he got the Empress down early on, became thrown out, let hounds slip him, lost the hunt or suffered any of the hundred and one misfortunes of a hunting day there were, as he knew, only too many ready to laugh behind their hands at him or recount gleefully over their dinner tables how he had failed in his task. Nor was his Imperial charge likely to be best pleased if any of these things happened. And, despite Spencer's assurances, he really had not the slightest idea if she could cross the country at all, especially at the places he intended to pick and the pace he intended to go.

When they went outside the best of the string she had brought with her and which had been ordered as her first horse was led forward by Bayzand. He bent down and put her up into the saddle. It was the first and last time that anyone other than Bay Middleton put her into the saddle when they were out together. Then they moved off, her horse going quietly and well under her light hands. Watching her with a critical eye he must have seen something to reassure him that she knew what she was about.

It did not at first, however, look as if they were going to have a good day. Several coverts were drawn blank. Then, suddenly, hounds opened on an outlier.

They were away in a flash, flying. Spencer saw to it that Bay had his start (it was one of the jealousies of the Pytchley that people said Spencer always saw to it that Bay had his start) and he was on their heels in an instant. In the same instant she was beside him. He had sworn to show her no quarter, nor did he. Hounds were screaming on a breast-high scent. He picked his place in the first fence that faced them, went at it and was over. She followed him without hesitation, sending her mount at the big stake-and-binder as if she had been doing it all her life. The only concession he paid her was to glance back as he landed to see if she was safely over. She was and was forging up to him again. They galloped for the next fence with the cry of hounds loud in both their ears. Before he had crossed two fields he knew he had a star on his hands.

For twenty-five minutes hounds fairly flew and for each of these minutes Middleton and the Empress had the best of it, riding out their hunt in the very first flight. He took the fences as they came and, giving him room only to get clear, she followed him. Once or twice indeed she pulled out to pick her own place and rose at the fence alongside him.

But her horse was nothing like as fit as he should have been for this sort of burst. He did not, after all, have a season's hard hunting inside him as had the mounts of Middleton and the other first flighters. Just at the end of it he failed to reach the far side of a ditch and drop, hit it and came down.

Middleton was back to her in an instant. As the horse floundered he plucked her out of the side-saddle and put her on her feet. When they got the horse up they found that the pummel of the saddle was broken. The fall could not have been other than a hard and heavy one. She had had a Spartan introduction to hunting in the Shires.

She was, however, unhurt. She was also quite unshaken. In fact she was flushed, radiant and grateful. She had seen someone doing supremely well what she had always wanted to do. She had experienced the thrill above all thrills which she had always desired, that of galloping and jumping at full stretch across English grass and over English fences. Gödollo was nothing to this!

She thanked him, laying her hand on his arm in that gesture she had when she wanted to express supreme gratitude or to plead for indulgence of a much desired wish. It was a gesture which never failed to move the Emperor. But the Emperor was a thousand miles away at his desk while his Imperial consort had just been picked out of a muddy ditch in Northamptonshire by an ex-Captain of cavalry and was realising, probably for the first time, what happiness and ecstasy were.

As for Middleton, from that moment he was in her thrall. So far from holding him back she had been alongside him most of the way and once or twice would have headed him had he let her. The sight of that feather-weight on the big blood horse, with her glorious hair and her lovely features alive with enjoyment, matching him jump for jump, was enough to set any man's pulses racing. There was to be no further talk of damning her eyes or of her interfering with his riding his own line. He was only too anxious to pilot her again if she would allow it. She for her part had no doubt that here at last she had found, at least so far as crossing a country went, the man she was looking for.

At first, however, events conspired against a repetition of that splendid day. Hunting arrangements had been made and even her wayward nature felt constrained to keep them. She was out with the Grafton next morning with a Colonel Pennant, a neighbour who was often at Easton Neston, piloting her, and the following day she was out again, this time with a Colonel Hunt who had been suggested much earlier as a permanent pilot, in charge.

That was four days' hard hunting in a row and one heavy fall. Gone now were the imagined illnesses, the vapours, the long spells of melancholia. She was tireless; the longest day was never then too hard. On her second appearance with the Grafton she rode her horse to a standstill just before hounds ran out of scent, but she was one of the only three with them at the time, the others being Colonel Pennant and Frank Beers, the huntsman. 'I have not known a moment's fatigue,' she wrote gaily to the Emperor, while Countess Festetics noted despairingly in her diary that while some people rested occasionally, 'We hunt every day.'

In addition to meeting Middleton and showing the way with the Grafton it had indeed been a wonderful week for the Empress. There were private dinner parties in the evening at Easton Neston to which Middleton and Spencer were invited and plans were made for a return to the Pytchley. Everyone was polite and everyone was gay. Rightly, she believed herself to be loved and admired by these natural, uninhibited people, so like the Hungarians but with so much better sport at their disposal, who cut such a dash over a country and then looked so smart in their plain but beautifully cut evening clothes across the mahogany when hunting had finished for the day. It was all such a change from the ornate grandeurs and falsities of the court in Vienna and the banquets where protocol laid down even the exact amount of wine to be consumed by each person. There uniforms and decorations glittered and the presence of the Emperor, 'The All-Highest' who felt it was required of him never to unbend, stultified conversation and enjoyment alike. Here there was Middleton at her side laughing and reliving the events of the day or Spencer telling of his protégé's latest prank and all of the company revelling in her beauty and complimenting her on her prowess in the chase.

But, unfortunately, she *was* the Empress of Austria; the great world and its protocol kept breaking in. However much she craved to be a private person she could not remain one for long. Queen Victoria profoundly disapproved both of the visit and its purpose. 'The Empress has been in England for a week and has taken a place in Northamptonshire merely for the hunting!' she recorded in her diary. Empresses, to her mind, did not behave thus frivolously. Nevertheless, having administered the first snub, duty now demanded that she should receive Elizabeth and an invitation was issued which almost amounted to a command. It was important then for diplomatic reasons that no further breach should occur between the two reigning ladies and the Emperor conveyed to Beust, the Austrian Ambassador to the Court of St James's, that the invitation should be accepted and the engagement kept. The unfortunate Beust was put to some considerable trouble in trying to arrange the matter with Nopsca, head of the Empress's household in England, for Elizabeth was extremely reluctant to go.

She was under other pressures, too. Like many another royal exile, the Queen of Naples was finding that money sufficient to keep up the state of life to which she was used was beginning to run short. Even in those days a hunting box in the Shires, twelve blood horses and a full staff of servants, grooms and second horsemen were all costly to maintain. She was anxious to curry favour with the Rothschilds and knew that that family longed to claim the recognition which entertaining the Empress would confer on them. She pressed her sister to visit them, holding out as a bait the prospect of a day's hunting with Mr Selby-Lowndes's Hounds.

In the end the Empress decided to combine both visits but she refused to stay the night at Windsor. Since she was determined not to lose a day's hunting she informed Queen Victoria she would arrive on Sunday 12 March. Where ceremony and protocol were concerned she was always capricious in the extreme. She sent off a series of conflicting messages to Windsor as to the time of her arrival and whether she would stay to luncheon or not. Since neither the Queen nor her court approved of Sunday visiting at any time all this did not augur well for the success of the meeting.

Church service at Windsor was at twelve. The Bishop of

Peterborough was sent for by the Queen and warned that on this Sunday he must on no account preach a long sermon. Just as he had mounted the steps of the pulpit, however, a page slipped in to whisper to Her Majesty that the Empress's arrival was imminent. 'This', noted the Queen grimly in her diary, 'was somewhat disconcerting.'

When she went down in person to the door to receive the Empress the Queen found that snow had commenced to fall and that her unpredictable guest, who was 'looking very handsome in black, with fur', had changed her mind again and would not now stay to luncheon. There was a flurry of introductions and presentations and then the Empress was off once more after a visit lasting precisely three-quarters of an hour which cannot have done much to improve relations between the two reigning houses. 'She spoke with delight', the Queen wrote afterwards in her diary, 'of having hunted each day since she arrived!! and of how civil everyone was. The Queen of Naples her sister is also in the neighbourhood for the same purpose. In spite of every offer she would neither remain to luncheon nor take anything.'

Elizabeth really had been uncommonly rude, but then that was her way. The old Queen bored her as did her stuffy courtiers; she hated ceremonial and she had not forgotten the earlier refusal to receive her. To make matters worse and to give more publicity to the whole affair the train bearing her and her suite back to London broke down in the snow and the stationmaster had to provide her with luncheon—and a bottle of claret—on a tray in her carriage. Then, to cap her indiscretions as it were, on the following day she paid a full and formal visit to Baron Ferdinand de Rothschild at Leighton House, riding over to Mentmore with him to inspect his stud. Hunting was impossible owing to the snow but it cleared the next morning so she returned to sample the sport with Mr Selby-Lowndes's Hounds. She could scarcely have been more tactless had she tried.

The visit over, she returned with delight to Easton Neston and the company of her suite and her English friends whom she was now calling her 'colony'. These included Mr John Elliott, who piloted the Queen of Naples, the Pennants and, of course, Spencer and Bay Middleton.

Very soon she began to realise that the horses she had brought with her were not up to their job. Mr Elliott was asked to cast his eye over them. He told her bluntly that only four of them were fit to be ridden over an English country the way she rode them and that the rest were useless. Middleton's advice on replacements was sought and gladly given. He himself had twenty hunters in his stables 'as good and clever as any man need wish to ride'. Some of these were called into service to fill the vacant places in her string and on one of them, Merry Andrew, she followed him through a terrific thirty minutes at racing pace from Barrington Gorse. 'None of *your* horses', she wrote to the unfortunate Emperor, 'are any good, they are slow and spiritless; one wants quite different material here.'

It did not bother her at all that her Sunday visit to the Queen, its abrupt termination and the sequel of luncheon in the train might have reached the Emperor's ears and caused him concern. In fact these events, together with her honouring the Rothschilds with a much longer stay than that given to their monarch, had made something of a stir in the court circles of both countries. So persistent was the talk and gossip that the question of an official denial of the wilder stories was taken up by Sir Henry Ponsonby, Queen Victoria's Private Secretary, with the British Ambassador in Vienna. 'I am glad to say that there has never been any idea here that the Empress was not offered luncheon at Windsor,' was the reply. 'The church story has not however been spoken of here and I have only acquainted Count Andrassy with it, as if it got about, the papers would get hold of it and things would be said which would be painful to the Emperor—in the higher reaches of Vienna society her spending a day at a 'Jew's' is harshly criticised. I have mentioned to Count Andrassy the English popular feeling against Sunday visiting and he would easily be able to suggest the inexpediency of another taking place.'

The likelihood of another taking place was remote in the extreme. Elizabeth was enjoying herself far too much and, now that she was properly mounted, she and Middleton were together cutting such a swathe across the Pytchley country as to astound all those who saw them.

She began to call him 'Bay'. The word came soft and sweetly

from her lips and appeared to be spoken with a particular affection. No one could deny the rapport they had established in the hunting field for it was there for all to see. Off it, too, some strange magnetism of shared danger and delight was drawing them together.

But the visit was a comparatively short one and the wonderful days were racing by. She crammed everything she could into them, hunting six days a week and going up to the Pytchley whenver opportunity offered. She was tanned and happy and laughing at her friends and herself, their adventures and misadventures. 'Count Wolkenstein', she wrote to Ida Ferenczy, 'fell twice in succession and came out of a swampy brook in such a state that his grey horse looked black and he himself like a Moor.' Even Rudolph got a letter—in Hungarian. 'I could not manage to write to you yesterday because I had to go to the Meet which took place a long way away. Aunt Marie (the Queen of Naples) rode my good bay horse and it went extremely well. Today and tomorrow there is no hunting in my part of the country because of the big races at Northampton but as there is no steeplechase I am not going.'

In fact the hunting season was ending and the point-to-point season beginning. Bay's thoughts and his horses were turning from hunting to racing. Although never in the very first flight of Gentlemen Riders he enjoyed considerable success on his own horses, mostly in point-to-points, where his wonderful eye for a natural country enabled him to seize opportunities for making up or saving ground not apparent to his fellows. Here, as in every other walk in life, he was intensely competitive. He rode with one object only in view—to carry his colours (black, pink hoops, black cap) to victory, and Arthur Yates, who was one of his less than whole-hearted admirers, has recorded that he did not much like either himself or his horses being beaten.

Beaten he was, however, the first time she saw him ride in a race. This was at the Pytchley point-to-point at Hopping Hill on 18 March. Spencer had erected a special pavilion to entertain her and her suite before racing began. Middleton was one of the very few outside the immediate Imperial circle asked to the luncheon which was reported to be 'on the most magnificent scale, carried out to perfection by Mr Hands the House Steward'.

He finished down the field on his own Musketeer in the Sportsman's Plate won by Mr Battam's most appropriately named Empress. The best he could do at the meeting was to gain third place in the Selling Stakes 'of 2 sovs with 30 sovs added' riding Spencer's brown mare Aurora and carrying 3lb overweight.

So delighted was the Empress with the day's sport that she decided to establish a meeting of her own to be called The Grafton Hunt Steeplechases. With the assistance of Spencer and Middleton a course was laid out in Easton Neston park. A stand was erected for privileged guests and, most important of all, she sent once more to Hancocks for a cup. Hancocks, now 'By Appointment to His Imperial Majesty The Emperor of Austria', designed and constructed a magnificent trophy. It was to be presented by herself in person and to be known as The Hohenembs Cup. She also laid down the conditions. The race was to be confined to horses from the packs she had hunted with during her stay, the Grafton, Bicester, Pytchley and Mr Selby-Lowndes's; weights were to be 13st and the distance three miles. Captain Middleton entered Musketeer for this race.

Unlike Spencer's strictly reserved luncheon for the high *ton* at Hopping Hill, the Empress entertained all who had helped her during her stay from the highest to the lowest in a special tent before racing. Champagne flowed, corks popped and with Middleton on one side and Spencer on the other she presided, happy, gay and vivacious, charming everyone by her presence.

The Hohenembs Cup, the chief race, was the second on the card. There were ten runners. British Yeoman, the favourite, who had run well at Newport Pagnall the week before, refused at the first fence. Middleton lay handy, tracking the leaders most of the way. The second last was a big brook. Middleton came cracking down into this, sent Musketeer sailing at it and gained lengths in his jump. Before the last he had overtaken the leader. He jumped this clear and went on to win comfortably by three lengths to the open delight of the Empress and the crowd.

Then she had the joy of presenting her cup to him amidst a storm of cheering, which went on and on. Whatever her faults, and they were many, she had the power of capturing the hearts of simple people, for when she was happy she was simple herself. And always she was utterly without pretension, grandeur or the Habsburg delusion that they were a caste set apart by the Almighty. As Middleton went down the steps of the little dais with the cup in his hands the cheering continued, for there were few there who did not realise that if she had won their hearts he had won at least a portion of hers.

She had presented a cup in a race the conditions of which were drawn up by herself at a meeting she had originated and the one man she wanted to win had won it. It was a wonderful note on which to end her visit.

Two days later she had gone, travelling to Vienna by way of Brussels, back from the fresh air and freedom to the court life and ceremonial she hated so much. Franz Joseph was touchingly delighted to have her back. He was proud, too, of her triumphs and, on hearing from Nopsca that 'Neither in England nor anywhere else in the world was there a lady who could ride like Her Majesty, and very few men either', he paid the expenses of her visit without demur. They amounted to 106,516 gulden, 93 kroner, about £120,000 in present day currency.

There was another consolation for her too and something to anticipate with pleasure and joy. Middleton had been invited to Gödollo for the commencement of the coming season and had accepted.

CHAPTER FIVE

Gödollo

The house party for the hunting at Gödollo that year was large and mixed. The Emperor himself was there along with Rudolph, now aged eighteen. Rudolph was precocious both sexually and mentally; he was attractive in manner when he wished, handsome, sulky and rebellious. He hated horses and the swaggering ways of those who rode them which seemed to him, as it has seemed to others before and since, to give them an unjustified acceptance of their own superiority. The Kinskys and Esterhazy, and Middleton when he arrived, largely ignored him. He had inherited from his mother a total inability to overlook or forget any insult, imagined or otherwise. The refusal of her friends to accept him into their own close coterie together with the indiscriminate reading which had been rammed undigested into his head was already beginning to turn his thoughts towards the liberalism he later displayed. Rudolph was never a true liberal; no one with Habsburg blood in their veins could be that. He took up the radical cause to avenge himself for the slights he thought he had been subjected to in his youth and to compensate for other qualities, such as courage, lacking within him. It must be said, however, that as he grew older, whatever motives had originally inspired him, his brains and position did help to advance the spread of new ideas and to counter-balance to some small degree the ingrained ultra-conservatism of his father.

The young Charles Kinsky, son of Prince Ferdinand, was included in the party for the first time. Kinsky was a year younger than Rudolph and was everything that the Crown Prince was not. Eager, dashing, a thruster to hounds, already searching for his first ride in a steeplechase, he was accepted immediately into the Empress's inner court. 'I did not form a good opinion of the Crown Prince then,' he wrote. 'He seemed to me to be opposing for the sake of opposing.' Much later, indeed too late, he came to change his view of Rudolph but it may be accepted that at the time the two young men of such widely differing tastes took an immediate dislike to each other, to the increase of Rudolph's sulks and discomfiture.

There was another guest, too, who brought with her potential for disquiet and disaster. Marie Wallersee was the Empress's niece. She had been born illegitimate, the result of an affair between Duke Ludwig of Bavaria, Elizabeth's brother, and the actress Henriette Mendel. The union was legitimised six months after her birth by the morganatic marriage between the pair. Henriette Mendel was given the courtesy title of Baroness Wallersee. Marie was eighteen years old and, as a horsewoman, second only to the Empress herself. In addition she was a pretty, intriguing little minx with, like Rudolph, a feeling of resentment against the world, hers being caused by the social slur of her illegitimacy and her parents' morganatic marriage. She was taken up by the Empress partly from genuine kindness and partly from admiration for her horsemanship. She won the Empress's confidence and, later, in the matter of Mayerling, betrayed it. The years following that tragedy dealt unkindly with Marie Wallersee and the verdict of history has been no less harsh, but the Empress herself scarcely displayed either understanding or compassion the following year when she married her off in a hurry to the uncouth Georg Larisch. Countess Festetics, observing the growing intimacy between niece and aunt and possessive and spiteful as ever, wrote in her diary a famous passage about Marie Wallersee which has often been quoted to display her insight into those surrounding the Empress: 'I would like to be her friend, I like her sometimes, but—but what? Something holds me back, I hardly dare put it down in case I am doing her a wrong. I have a feeling—I'll put it delicately—that she is not genuine, not sincere, as though she had an acting talent.'

All the old faithfuls, Rudi Liechtenstein, Nicky Esterhazy, Andrassy, the other Larischs, Johann and his son Heinrich, were there too. Since every one of these men was to one degree or another in love with his beautiful hostess the atmosphere at Gödollo that summer was, it may be imagined, somewhat overheated and explosive. The arrival of Middleton at the beginning of the cub-hunting season did little to lower the temperature or lessen the tension. In fact, of course, it heightened it, for all of them reacted to him in their different ways.

The Empress was obviously thrilled and delighted to see him again. Nicky Esterhazy was jealous and glowering, Charles Kinsky conceived for him an immediate hero-worship which he never lost, Rudi Liechtenstein preserved the calm and smiling acceptance with which he met everything. Marie Wallersee, who was prepared to fall in love with any personable man at least for a short time, fell in love with him, and Franz Joseph did not know what to make of him at all.

It has been said, with total inaccuracy, that the Empress treated Middleton like a groom. She did not but the Emperor did, or very nearly. English society was always an utter mystery to continental courts and dynasties. They could not grasp that it was founded on a comparatively loosely interwoven system of classes and that entry into the higher echelons was, broadly speaking, governed by money and land. Those who owned sufficient of either found almost every gate opened to them, especially at a time when the ranks were widening and Edward, Prince of Wales, with his fondness for what the continentals considered to be parvenus and jews, was the social arbiter.

In direct contrast European aristocracy—which found its apex in the Habsburgs—was founded on caste and that caste was governed by blood, birth and quarterings. To Franz Joseph in his position as All Highest, Middleton, lacking any quarterings, would have had no pretensions to the purple at all. Indeed it must have seemed to the Emperor, from his lofty eminence, and ignorant as he was of the conventions of English hunting, that by accepting the post of pilot to the Empress this young soldier occupied a position almost analogous to Allen and Holmes.

Franz Joseph housed him in a small cottage a little distance away from the palace and treated him as something in the nature of a court jester, neither whose jokes nor whose language he understood but at whom and with whom he was content to laugh. Never a man of any percipience or understanding where people were concerned, it was inconceivable to him that his wife could display any closer interest in Middleton than she had in Allen, Holmes or Bayzand.

This was a situation the Empress knew very well how to exploit. Almost from his arrival she made a point of having Middleton to herself, though occasionally Marie Wallersee was allowed to accompany them on her rides. Very often, however, the threesome did not last for long, Marie being despatched on trivial errands soon after they started out. All this, naturally enough, did not go unnoticed.

But if Middleton puzzled the Emperor he himself must have found the society into which he had been plunged equally strange if not, indeed, to some degree almost comic. In the first place the male members of the party with any claim to military rank invariably wore uniform on all occasions, even when hunting. The Emperor himself usually wore an undress white tunic and red cavalry trousers. He made an exception to this when he went shooting. Then he donned what must have seemed to Middleton's conventional English eyes a suit of quite extraordinary tweeds, or lederhosen. Rudolph, too, was always in uniform, ostentatiously stalking about in the blue trousers of the infantry to show that he took their side in the increasing social and military rivalry between the two arms of the service. All this could not but have seemed strange to Middleton or to any English soldier, whose one ambition was to get out of uniform and into civilian clothes as soon as he decently could.

Dinners, too, were glittering, full-dress affairs presided over with great pomp by the Emperor and ruled by the strictest protocol before, during and after the meal. Sometimes, however, the Empress in her impulsive fashion would decree an early supper to be taken by herself and her own inner court of whom Middleton was invariably one. These were usually held on hunting days soon after they had bathed and changed when, in all the intimacy of shared sport and danger, the Empress tried to re-create the atmosphere she had known and loved at Easton Neston. On these occasions the Emperor would be left to dine alone with the remnants of the household. She was the mistress of Gödollo and there no one, not even the Emperor, could interfere with her.

These *dîners intimes* and Middleton's privileged position at them stirred up a hot-bed of intrigue of which the Emperor was quite unaware. Nicholas Esterhazy, who had fancied himself as Elizabeth's right hand man until Middleton came along, grew more lowering every day. Out hunting Middleton, with the young Charles Kinsky copying him, cheerfully overrode hounds and got heartily cursed for his pains. Others, not too sorry to see Esterhazy's nose put out of joint, criticised his handling of the hounds and asked Middleton's advice. The Baltazzis, Alexander and Hector, came out hunting too. Since they could, of course, speak perfect English they became friendly with Middleton and this, coupled with the glamour surrounding their recent Derby victory with Kisber in June and the fact that Hector was now riding winners all over the place, raised them to instant favouritism in the eyes of the Empress. They, too, were asked to Gödollo and brought their sister, Baroness Vetsera, along with them. The invitation was much criticised, especially in court circles in Vienna. The Baltazzis had, of course, no quarterings and the higher circles in Vienna absolutely denied them entrance. The invitation, too, put Nicky Esterhazy into a further quandary for Baroness Vetsera was widely said to be or to have been his mistress. All this meant nothing to the Empress. A Russian diplomat, surveying the whole scene with an amused and dispassionate eye wrote home about the Baltazzis: 'They are called "rastas" by those who dislike them because of their push and dash. But the horse, one knows, is an aristocratic animal, with the power of conferring nobility.' Certainly Middleton's friendship did no harm to their ambitions and, equally certainly, they were intelligent enough to cultivate it. It was during that season at Gödollo that Rudolph first met the family and the first faltering steps on the road to Mayerling were taken.

Further to stir things up a hunting couple arrived from England. These have remained unnamed but were probably the Pennants who had been so kind to Elizabeth during her stay in England. She had a habit of repaying kindnesses with invitations to Gödollo and subsequently—as in this case—regretting them. For the Pennants profoundly disapproved of her association with Middleton and were unwise enough to say so in the presence of Marie Wallersee who promptly carried the tale back. As a result the couple were barred from the Empress's presence and the *dîners intimes*. Instead they had to suffer the formalities of the Emperor's table. He himself, poor man, was even more puzzled by them and their correct place in society than he was by Middleton. He could not understand a word they said and was bored by the way they said it. Finally he issued an edict banning them from his table and they left.

In the end, things came to such a pass between Middleton and Esterhazy that Esterhazy resigned the Mastership in a huff. Then came the problem of replacing him which entailed the usual discussions, intrigues and scheming for support. The Emperor had no influence here. The pack was controlled by the Empress and her friends. She was vastly amused by it all. 'Everybody wishes to be Master', she exclaimed gaily to Andrassy, 'just as in a Ministry everybody wishes to be President.'

The turn-out of the Gödollo Hounds was not in accordance with the highest standards of the Shires. This may have had something to do with one or two of Middleton's outspoken remarks which, duly carried back, had upset Esterhazy. The Master and hunt servants wore green coats, the field either the conventional scarlet and top hat or, if they were soldiers, uniform. On the occasions when the Emperor hunted, since he thought the scarlet coat to be the uniform of the day, he wore it. His enjoyment of the chase cannot, however, have been increased by the fact that Elemer Batthyany, son of the executed Count Ludwig, was also a member of the field. As a revenge for the Emperor's failure to pardon his father Elemer had sworn never to recognise him. Whenever the All Highest appeared at the meet, therefore, Batthyany would ostentatiously doff his hat to the Empress in recognition and obeisance to her as Queen of Hungary and then, equally ostentatiously, turn his back on her husband and ride away.

The sight of officers in helmets and gentlemen with their whips pushed into the tops of their boots must have astonished and affronted Middleton, and indeed helmets cannot have been the most comfortable things to fall into. There was, however, precious little falling or the risk of it. An English ambassador, asked for a day's hunting at Gödollo a year or so later, wrote to his wife: 'It is delicious ground to ride over, all sandy fields, except when you come near a bog, and then you must look out

. . . but there is practically no jumping, a few little ditches now and then.' To a man accustomed to 'the cream of the cream in the Shire of the Shires' it would have seemed scarcely hunting at all. But, of course, there was the consolation of her company, for they were everywhere together. She took him to see the stud farms at Kisber, where the Derby winner had been bred, and Kladrub. Middleton was given a mount in an amateur steeplechase at the Pardubitz meeting and they drove over to it together.

She must have longed to see him repeat his victory in the Hohenembs Cup here, on her own ground. He looked like doing it, too, coming over the last fence. Then the young Charles Kinsky, riding his first race, came at him with a rush. In a desperate finish Kinsky got up to beat his hero by a head. He was to ride against Middleton often again in England later on, success sometimes going one way then the other, but he always maintained that Middleton was never as good between the flags as in the hunting field and that he could not ride an effective finish. At all events he was excited and thrilled by his victory then and delighted at the congratulations Middleton and the Empress heaped upon him.

There is evidence that Elizabeth was puzzled by the fascination Middleton had for her. Although she was 'the loveliest crowned head in Europe' and, along with Queen Victoria, the most important in prestige and position, power and social distinction did not come into her thoughts at all. She had none of the Habsburg consciousness of their own unique creation. There was in her too much of her father and his amiable mockery of rank and position for that. But she did recognise that she was drawn to Middleton by something outside her ordinary sphere of experience, that their lives, backgrounds and indeed their natures, save in so far as horses were concerned, seemed utterly irreconcilable. Indeed even where horses were concerned there were differences, for her control of them was won by understanding, his by mastery.

The story that she was found gazing at a picture of Titania and the ass murmuring 'Bay and I' may well be true. Certainly when she was asked how they managed to communicate since he was deaf and her voice so soft she answered that it did not matter, they managed well enough. That there was some unspoken bond between them which often exists between opposites is a fact and all who saw them together, especially in the hunting field, recognised it. That they were not then lovers in the physical sense of the word is equally certain.

As a woman Elizabeth was sexually shy and cold; as a man Bay was neither. But the Victorian upper class kept the rules they, or their caste, laid down. Certain types of women—loose married women and the lower orders—were fair game. Single girls and those who proclaimed themselves inaccessible were not.

Elizabeth came into the latter class and for them an entirely different set of rules applied. These women were elevated to realms of purity to which perhaps even they themselves did not always aspire. They were made the subject of romantic love, mystic, wonderful, a counter-balance to the earthy lusts indulged in elsewhere. Elizabeth was well suited to play just this part in Middleton's life. She was high-born and beautiful, an object of adoration not desire, a wayward, unpredictable goddess who touched the earth lightly and who carried something ethereal with her as she went. Consciously or unconsciously she capitalised all this. She knew now she could bend men to her will and she loved to exercise that power. By yielding she would lose it. She wanted to and did remain a fairy princess.

On his part, too, the ethereal plane on which their association had so far been conducted could not but have had its attractions. The idea of pure romance was never very far away from the Victorian male ethos. In those days men could and did go to their graves having conducted for years high-flown platonic love affairs which would be considered ludicrous by all but a very few today. These romantic liaisons soon became known and recognised as in the instance of Oliver Montagu and Queen Alexandra. In some way it gave the male party an extra cachet, an additional air of remoteness and glamour and set him as a man slightly apart, almost as though he wore on his sleeve an oriflamme of renunciation.

But romantic love, however purely conceived, brings in its train its own stresses and problems. The men who conducted these high-flown affairs were for the most part hard-riding cavaliers, full of fire and dash and hot red blood. Gallantry alone was not enough. There was almost always another, seamier side to Victorian high romance.

London abounded then in brothels of every sort catering for all varieties of sexual taste. Under a spurious cloak of secrecy and hypocrisy they were patronised by the wealthy, the well-born and the fashionable. The 'pretty horse-breakers' of Rotten Row and St John's Wood gained a universal recognition that almost bordered upon respectability.

The tantalising presence of this lovely creature constantly beside him, sometimes showing off her horses for him in her *manège*, sometimes fencing with foil and épée before him in dresses that came close to *déshabilles*, must have been torture to Middleton. 'I could watch you forever,' he is said to have muttered under his breath after one of these fencing sessions. Her niece, too, commented that she was not surprised there was talk amongst the suite in view of the costumes her aunt wore on these occasions.

There can be no question but that Elizabeth liked putting men through their paces almost as much as she did horses. It is probable that this trait was latent in her always, as it is in many women, and that the rupture of her marriage together with the reason for it developed and intensified her desire to stir men without satisfying them. It almost certainly led up to what was the most bizarre incident in the association between her and Middleton.

Towards the end of his stay at Gödollo Middleton expressed his desire to go into Budapest and see something of the city. This was agreed and one of her personal suite was deputed by the Empress to accompany him as interpreter and guide.

Once they reached the city Middleton appears to have been determined to give his guardian the slip. Promising to meet him later on at the casino he went off on his own. Whether he was acting on prior information from his sporting friends or whether the homing instinct of the Victorian man-about-town for those places where sexual gratification could be obtained directed his footsteps, it is of course impossible to say. The fact remains, however, that he found his way to the house of 'a charming lady of indefinite social position'.

The rendezvous at the casino was not kept by Middleton. The member of the suite, after waiting for hours, determined that his best course was to return to Gödollo without his charge. He did so in some trepidation and his report threw the palace into an uproar. Visions of assault, abduction and even murder of her favourite flashed through the Empress's volatile mind. Next morning things were no better for there was still no information as to the missing man's whereabouts or what had happened to him. The Empress was about to request that the whole security services of the nation be employed in the search when a telegram arrived. It was from the Chief of Police in Budapest and stated baldly that Middleton was in the principal police station, quite safe but penniless.

Exact details of what occurred remain, naturally enough, obscure. It appears, however, that Middleton, probably through ignorance of the language, for in England a man of his experience would hardly have allowed himself to be hoaxed in such a way, permitted his pretty lady to lead him to what he assumed to be her boudoir but turned out to be a thieves' kitchen. The adventure took up the best part of the night and, by the time he made his escape, presumably, knowing him, having left his mark on anyone who sought to detain him, all his money was gone. Deciding that the only place for a man in his situation to go to was the nearest police station he made his way to it and explained his predicament as best he could. The telegram was then immediately despatched to Gödollo. On its arrival another equerry was sent to bring him back.

The sexual overtones of the exploit were unavoidable. The Emperor roared with laughter when it was told to him. This was just the sort of earthy escapade he enjoyed. And after all the fellow belonged to that strange—to his eyes—indeterminate English hunting and racing caste from which this sort of thing might well be expected. That was not the way, however, in which the Empress saw it. She was furious. It must have seemed to her an affront to her beauty and fascination that a man close to her whom she certainly admired and in her own way loved at least a little, had betrayed both himself and their association in a sordid sexual adventure. It could not have done other than remind her of the traumas she had suffered from the Emperor's infidelities years before. She allowed her displeasure to be seen in no mistaken fashion. Middleton was out of favour and Nicky Esterhazy temporarily taken back to be *maître en titre* in name if not in fact.

But Bay Middleton possessed something the Emperor totally lacked—charm. He could turn a story against himself into laughter and laugh with those who laughed at him, and he could make a sorry episode into something amusing and gay. This is what he now set out to do and, being Middleton, he succeeded. It is indeed a sign of the affection in which Elizabeth held him that she, who never forgave, in no time at all had forgiven him and had turned her favour back to him again. Their intimate rides together were resumed to the open fury of Esterhazy and others who had sought to profit from Middleton's fall from grace.

But the golden days at Gödollo were running out. Middleton's visit drew to a close. The days, the drives, the visits to the stud farms and great estates, the hunts across the *putsa*, all sped by and suddenly were gone.

She was in tears when he left though her emotions were concealed from the Emperor. For another meeting seemed, and indeed was, a long way off.

CHAPTER SIX

'Be with them I will!'

After Bay's departure even Gödollo, the beloved place, carried its emptiness and unhappiness with it. But the fox-hunting and riding continued. Nicky Esterhazy, like many another MFH who has resigned in a fit of pique, took back the hounds and Marie Wallersee continued to ingratiate herself in the Empress's favour. She was pretty and vivacious and a beautiful horsewoman. She alone was entrusted with the Empress's best horses when her aunt could not ride. She schooled the circus horses and rode the hunters to hounds. She was cheerful and gay, pretty and pert; she raised the Empress's spirits and became an ever closer confidante.

As well as her other qualities Marie Wallersee had some slight talent for caricature and her sketches, tinged with touches of friendly malice, were exactly calculated to entertain the Empress. One such depicted her aunt in a riding habit after a fall, her silk hat battered and awry on her head. One one side of her stood Bay Middleton, on the other Nicky Esterhazy. Both were endeavouring to help her to her feet and were pulling her asunder in the process.

The Empress was delighted with the drawing. Laughingly saying that it almost amounted to *lèse majesté* she declared her intention of sending it to Bay. It is probable that she did do this for she was a compulsive letter-writer and wrote constantly to Middleton during their periods of separation. After his marriage these letters were destroyed by Charlotte, his wife. On his side the correspondence was said to have been conducted through a lady-in-waiting, though which one is not known.

Unquestionably he was much in her thoughts that winter.

She still longed for the pace and thrill of English fox-hunting and the gaiety that went with it. Of all these things she had had a brief glimpse with him the season before and she badly wanted to return and savour them more fully. But she was now approaching her forties. Time was beginning to run out for her and she knew it. Almost desperately she sought to retain her youth by preserving the graceful lines of her body. Gymnastic apparatus accompanied her wherever she went and she spent hours on exercises aimed to preserve the slimness of her lovely figure. Her latent narcissism increased as she grew older and her face was daily and minutely scrutinised for any sign that the years were leaving their mark.

That winter, determined, indeed almost desperate, to preserve her loveliness both for herself and for those few upon whom she cared to cast its glow, she resorted to quite extraordinary reducing and cosmetic preparations which were made up for her by specialists under her personal direction. If her skin had been exposed to the sun for any time at all a mask of honey, carefully purified, or potcheese as a variant, was applied to her face and left there for at least two hours. A hair shampoo was made up of a mixture which combined pressed onions, cognac and Peru balsam. For massage another special lotion comprising ox-gall, alcohol and glycerine was used. During the hunting season or if she was riding every day this was varied by yet another special receipt of her own known as her 'muscle water'. She was convinced that this relaxed all body tensions after exercise and so proud of it was she that barrels of this strange love potion were actually shipped to England for the personal use of Captain Middleton.

The Queen of Naples was fascinated by all this and borrowed certain of her sister's cosmetic aids, but even she baulked at 'the gladiator's bath'. This had originated in Corfu and consisted of a special oil heated almost to boiling point and mixed with the hottest bath water the occupier could stand. 'I am neither a sardine nor an old leather saddle to be preserved in oil,' the Queen told her sister in her tart way when offered one of these baths.

The Empress's preparations for and hopes of an early return to the Shires early in 1877 were dashed by a worsening of Imperial relations with England. The situation did not make even an incognito visit propitious and her plans had to be abandoned.

She was bored in Vienna and a move to Gödollo, did not seem, for once, to help. Symptoms of melancholia and nervous trouble began to return.

Then, at Gödollo, she found herself confronted with a domestic problem, or she imagined she did, for much of it may have been of her own creation.

Marie Wallersee, like many other attractive minxes of her sort, could not meet a man without imagining he was in love with her, nor could she prevent herself setting her cap at him. Elemer Batthyany, Nicky Esterhazy and Aristide Baltazzi were only three of the many men she fancied were helplessly in her toils. They all happened to be members of the hunt and of the Empress's immediate circle and all, at least to some extent, under her spell. It was both irritating and annoying for her to have her niece openly proclaiming their capture.

This was bad enough but then Marie began to pursue the Crown Prince. Rudolph made his dislike for the girl quite clear. But Rudolph was a devious man, given to saying one thing and meaning another and to cloaking his real feelings under a screen of secrecy and deception. One of his tutors, Latour, had, whilst he was growing up, written of him to the Emperor: 'I have already told your Majesty that the Crown Prince does not tell direct untruths but has repeatedly expressed opinions which I know he does not hold or which are even the reverse of his true opinion.' If he were, in fact, to be attracted now or in the future terrible complications would arise, for a marriage between the heir to the Habsburg Empire and the daughter of a morganatic union actually born illegitimate was inconceivable.

Elizabeth did not want to lose the girl from her entourage for she was far too useful as a confidante and adorer, a bearer of messages and, at times, a tactful chaperone. A *mariage de convenance* and a quick one was the obvious and immediate solution. The Empress's choice fell upon the twenty-two-year-old Georg Larisch, cousin and brother-in-law of Count Heinrich Larisch who was, of course, a close friend and prominent member of her suite.

Marie was packed off to Castle Solza, the gloomy home of the family. There, under the unsympathetic and determined eye of Countess Festetics, to whose care she had been entrusted for the visit, a marriage was duly arranged.

The betrothal took place on 8 September and the couple—they could hardly be described as 'happy' since they appear to have disliked each other at first sight and forever afterwards—were married at Gödollo six weeks later in the presence of the Emperor and the Empress.

Even the hard-hearted Festetics was moved to pity at the sight of the girl's evident unhappiness. She had never cared for Marie Wallersee and made no secret of it. Disliking her as she did, however, she was still moved to make some slight protest concerning the whole affair to her mistress. If others approved the marriage then Marie should be content with it too, was the cold reply and neither she nor anyone else ever received another word of explanation from the Empress as to her conduct in the matter. Elizabeth could be utterly ruthless where the feelings of others were concerned if they touched upon her own plans and what she conceived to be her chances of happiness.

Already, at that time, she saw a way beginning to open for her return to England. The Crown Prince figured in her plans, as did Marie whom she wished to accompany her. Marie, single and up to mischief with any man she could lay her eyes upon but especially Rudolph, would be a grave embarrassment; but Marie safely married off and no permanent danger to any man, was a very different proposition. When the girl left for her honeymoon Elizabeth mentioned the prospect of a trip to the Shires and the hope that she and her husband would come in her suite. It must have been the only moment of happiness that the unfortunate Marie Wallersee knew during those ghastly few weeks. Foolish as she undoubtedly was and knavish though she later became, she scarcely deserved this treatment.

Relations between England and the Empire were on the mend. They had been steadily improving for months. Because it now affected her personally and her plans and intentions, Elizabeth, for once, had her ear to the political ground. Timing her moment to a nicety she pressed on the Emperor the fact that Rudolph's education would be incomplete without a visit to examine the expanding economic power of Great Britain and to see how that country's interests were advanced through trade in the councils of the world. It would also, she added, be most suitable were she to accompany Rudolph and she could combine this with some hunting in the Shires. The Emperor, who never understood either his wife or his son, agreed; but busy as he was with his unending paper-work and the vast problems that beset him, he may not have realised just to what he was consenting.

Immediately the Empress began to put her well-laid plans into effect. Middleton was instructed to see to the purchase of a stud of blood horses suitable to carry a lady in the front rank with the Pytchley. Middleton and Spencer both lived in the Pytchley country and it was unthinkable now that she should have her residence anywhere else but near those two close friends and boon companions. Linger, her secretary, was told to negotiate for a hunting box. With Spencer's assistance the choice fell on Cottesbrooke Park, a few miles from Althorp.

The prospect of the best part of a full season's hunting in England banished the melancholia like mist before the morning sun. Christmas was spent at Gödollo in joyful anticipation. Immediately afterwards the whole party left for England.

Middleton, meanwhile, during their enforced separation, had been consolidating his position as the hardest man to hounds in all the galloping countries. Superbly mounted, beautifully turned out, his eye for a country sharpened by his increasing knowledge of it, only one man came at all close to challenging his supremacy. This was Captain 'Doggie' Smith. A quieter character than Middleton and a far more retiring man, Smith was the better horseman of the two. Never as well mounted as his rival he yet managed to persuade whatever he rode into the front rank in any hunt. Portland, in comparing them in his recollections, remarked: 'I have frequently noticed that Doggie Smith and his mounts always appeared to be on good terms whereas I have seen Bay Middleton very much at difference with his. Doggie Smith went almost equally well on any class of horse; good, bad or indifferent, they made no difference to him.'

In many ways Middleton was a spoilt boy and behaved like one. But it was this very boyishness that saved him. Somewhere in that boyishness lay the charm that captured the Victorians who were extremely näive even when at their most sophisticated and who liked men to be boys at heart. 'He is only an overgrown boy,' the Empress remarked wistfully to

Marie Wallersee and here too that streak of boyishness may well have touched some chord of sympathy in one who was married to a man who had never been a boy at all.

During those months of separation the wild pranks for which he was famous continued. Lord Strathnairn, whom he had known in Ireland as Commander of the Forces, barricaded himself into his bedroom at Wentworth Wodehouse when Bay was a house guest to prevent some manic invasion late at night from his one-time subordinate. And the highly unlikely story began to circulate of Bay's betting a lady friend he would conceal himself in her bedroom where she could not find him. On retiring she searched the room without success until he finally disclosed himself hidden in her bolster.

With all this went other exploits and indiscretions which brought trouble in their train. One of these made a lifelong enemy of the Queen of Naples. Hearing that her sister would be absent from the hunting field for the 1876–77 season she conceived the idea that it would be pleasant for herself to be piloted by Captain Middleton. A number of the staff of the Austrian Embassy hunted regularly and she asked Beust, the Ambassador, to have one of these convey her wishes to Bay. She may have thought that this formal method of approach, having a hint of a command about it, was more likely to succeed than a personal one. If she did she was sadly in error. 'I'm damned if I'm going to pilot every damn Queen who comes to this country,' was the reply the emissary received. Once again the remark was too good not to be repeated. It came back quickly to the Queen of Naples' ears. Jealous already of her sister's success and sharing with her an unrelenting and unforgiving nature where a snub or a slight was concerned, she never forgave Middleton and her enmity was to have a disruptive effect on the Empress's happily planned and eagerly anticipated second visit.

Spencer's hero-worship and the favour he unquestionably showed Bay out hunting also brought envy and jealousy with them, for Bay was not the man to allow this to go unremarked. Portland, again, recorded that in his opinion Bay was not altogether as deaf as he sometimes pretended to be. He told how a story went the rounds that Bay, on one occasion, intent on securing his start failed to notice that hounds had thrown up on the far side of the first fence. As a result he jumped slap into the middle of them. 'Hold hard, Bay, hold hard,' Spencer shouted. Hounds opened again and began to run on. Scent was patchy and Bay did the same thing at the next fence. Seeing him riding at it and anticipating what was about to happen Spencer shouted: 'Hold hard, Bay! No, I mean *Captain* Middleton, hold hard! And if you jump into my hounds again I hope to goodness you get a fall and break your neck!' Middleton's horse did fall just as he landed in the middle of the pack. Spencer followed him. Dismounting, he took his friend's head in his hands calling out as he did so 'Oh, Bay! You know I didn't mean what I said; you haven't broken your neck, Bay, have you?' Victorian male friendships were nothing if not dramatic.

But there was another, quieter side to Middleton which should not be overlooked. The long evenings spent playing whist skilfully with such as Sir Chandos Leigh, who did not suffer fools gladly and who had forgiven and forgotten the coat-tail incident, have attracted little notice in the recollections of the period. They were unspectacular parts of a spectacular life and have therefore gone unrecorded. Nor have the instances of his thoughtfulness and kindliness received their due. One such was the occasion when he, along with a collection of companions, were guests at a hunting hotel where a lady and her mother were staying. The mother fell ill and the illness had become serious by the time Bay and his friends arrived. Her daughter had never actually met Middleton but she knew his reputation and this was enough to make her dread the probable effect the new arrivals' uproarious conduct would have on her mother's illness. In those days young ladies did not approach unattached men without an introduction. Summoning her courage, however, and rather dreading her reception, the girl made herself known to Middleton and explained the situation. The reply she received was that he had already learnt of her mother's condition and, on hearing of it, had issued instructions that there was to be no bear-fighting or disturbances of any sort during the stay and that, further, he would remove his boots whenever he passed her mother's door and would see to it that his friends did the same. The instructions were strictly carried out and the lady in question never forgot either the man or the incident.

This quality of compassion could suddenly and unexpectedly shine through the hard outer shell he presented to the world. Combined with his infectious gaiety and the aura of success surrounding him, it made him exceptional and explained his lasting attraction for such differing characters as Spencer and the Empress.

Spencer, as it happened, had not been well during the early part of that season. He had never been really physically robust; it was for reasons of health and in order to winter abroad that he had given up his first mastership of the Pytchley in 1864. Now the strain of hunting the two packs from Brigstock and Brixworth was telling on him despite the fact that he had a special lightweight brougham made to carry him to meets at a gallop. During November and most of December he remained in his villa in Florence while Mr Herbert Langham acted as Master and Goodall hunted the hounds. He had arranged, however, to return in time for the Empress's visit and he was back in Spencer House, St James's, on 28 December. The next day he travelled to Althorp where he proposed to spend the remainder of the season and to resume his Mastership.

The Empress—there was no question of an incognito this time—accompanied by Rudolph and their respective suites arrived at Victoria on Monday 31st. The Queen of Naples and Georg and Marie Larisch were on the platform to meet her. On arrival they drove to a small hotel in Brook Street which was her favourite in the city. It was called Claridge's and she was among the first of its many famous royal and fashionable visitors. She had not felt well on the train journey across Europe and had kept much to herself. That evening she dined alone with Rudolph and her household. The following morning after a quick visit to the Sisters of Charity of St Vincent de Paul in Carlisle Place, her health and spirits now completely restored, she was off in a special carriage on the twelve o'clock train bound for Northampton, Brixworth and Cottesbrooke Park.

Rudolph was left in London to pursue his own paths. Elizabeth knew that her son had neither the nerve nor the ability to ride in front in a Shire field. Since she had no intention of allowing him to disgrace both himself and her, before she left Austria she cautioned him against making the attempt: 'I shall certainly take good care not to take part in the hunts when I go to

England,' he wrote back to reassure her. 'Our people here do not see any great glory in breaking one's neck, and my popularity means too much to me that I should fling it away on things of this kind.'

Rudolph, in fact, was determined to use the visit to explore and investigate for his future use and Imperial education all the customs and technology of what was then the greatest country in the world. He also intended to exploit every opportunity for enjoyment, sexual or otherwise, which the capital city and the pleasure-loving society dominated by the Marlborough House set could offer. In this he was to have every assistance from the Master of his household (some called him his *maître de plaisir*), Captain Count Carl Bombelles. Like his father Rudolph had had an early initiation into the pleasures of sex. Under the tuition of Bombelles he had become a skilled and ardent lover, too ardent, in fact, for his own good, as events were tragically to show. The Prince of Wales, no laggard in these pursuits himself, is said to have been entertained by his sophistication and appreciative of his prowess.

Elizabeth cared nothing for any of this. Rudolph's visit provided a convenient cloak for her escape to the hunting countries and that, for her, was enough. Indeed throughout her life she gave little thought to him or any of her children save the youngest, Valerie, to whom she perhaps gave too much, except when, as in the affair of Gondrecourt, his best interests served also to advance her own ends. She was then just forty and looked at least ten years younger. 'Children', she had once said, 'are the curse of a woman, for when they come they drive away beauty which is the best gift of the gods.' Where she was going she was scarcely likely to relish the presence of a twenty-year-old son who, besides being a feeble horseman, had intellectual and liberal leanings and had already displayed his dislike for the Corinthians with whom she intended to mix.

To her unconcealed delight Spencer and Middleton were on the platform at Brixworth to greet her. Together they drove in Spencer's carriage to Cottesbrooke.

Cottesbrooke Park was not as grand as Easton Neston nor was it as large. It was a graceful, medium-sized Palladian mansion which had been built by the Langham family. The

Langham estates were then being administered by the Commissioners in Lunacy for the incumbent, Sir James Langham, was insane. Herbert Langham, who would succeed him, was glad enough to let the property to the Empress for the rent was enormous and his pretensions were far greater than his resources.

The accommodation in the house not being sufficient, some members of the suite had to be boarded out. Count and Countess Heinrich Larisch were at Guilsborough Grange. Prince Kinsky, Charles Kinsky's father, who had brought his English stud-groom, Reynolds, with him was at Brixworth. Here his son joined him for a short time, renewing his acquaintance with Middleton and having his first taste of English fences before being recalled to his regiment. There was a newcomer, too, Count Clam-Gallas, a friend of Rudi Liechtenstein, who was lodged with him at Wansford.

The stables, however, were all that could be desired. And it was to the stables that, in the company of Middleton, she immediately repaired on her arrival. Almost all the stud were new purchases. On her behalf Middleton had bought wisely and well. When it became known for whom he had been buying the price had gone up—at least fifty per cent one writer said. But, with an almost bottomless purse behind him, he had been able to go for the best and to get it. He gave up to five hundred pounds a horse, an enormous price in those days, and, wisely, had bought more on potential and performance than on appearance. He had cast his net wide in securing them for her and had crossed over to Ireland on some of his buying expeditions. One of the horses he bought there and which was to prove perhaps the most successful of them all, 'Bravo', had been first spotted for him in Meath by Mr George Darby, a well-known Northamptonshire dealer.

She was delighted with them all and said so. 'Remember', she added as they finished the inspection, laying her hand on his arm in the way she had, 'I do not mind the falls, but I will not scratch my face.' In fact, so well had he purchased and schooled her horses for her and so well did his eye and experience serve him that she went through the season without a fall. That year there were no complaints about the inadequacy of the horseflesh as on the previous visit, nor could even the Queen of Naples carp at his choice. One member of the Pytchley field said at the end of her stay that the horses Bay had bought for her would have been cheap had he paid the full five hundred for every one of them.

But the first day, at Yelvertoft, was a disappointment. Spencer could not come out since he was sitting as chairman of the quarter sessions at Northampton. Although Middleton piloted her as he did every day on that visit, there was precious little hunting for fog came down almost as soon as hounds moved off. A little later it became impenetrable and it was impossible to see the fences or anything else. The only consolation she had was that owing to the fog no one in the large crowd could stare at her and so there was no need to bring the fan into play.

The next day, from Harrington, was far better. They found almost immediately at Loatland Wood. Half the field were left but not Middleton and the Empress. The brook at Desborough stopped many of those who did get away with the hounds. Four of the first flighters went into it. Three of them were women, riding for their lives, as jealous as cats, out to show that others of their sex as well as this foreign royalty could cross a country at the top of the hunt. The Empress and Bravo skimmed over it like a bird.

With Desborough brook behind them hounds stuck to their fox and ran on a blazing scent. It was a stiff country and Middleton and the Empress did not quite have the best of it for Captain Fisher on his good grey is reported as the man who cut out the work. Middleton may not have been best pleased at this but just the same they were both there in the first flight all the way. Considering the stiffness of the country and that it was two years since she had faced these obstacles this was an achievement in itself. She was, of course, virtually no burden at all on a horse's back for her riding weight, including the cumbersome side-saddle of the day, only amounted to 8st 7lb. Bravo never made a mistake throughout the hunt. This was more than could be said for the mounts of others. Grief in plenty came to even the select few left in it after the brook had thinned the ranks. Mrs Oliver, trying to catch up, had a fall on the road and was rendered unconscious; Count Clam-Gallas turned over at some stiff timber, broke his jaw and he, too, was unconscious when they picked him up. He was taken back to Cottesbrooke and carried into the house under the horrified eyes of Countess Festetics who suffered paroxysms of anxiety every time her mistress went out. She had reason to do so for the chronicler of this hunt, after giving details of these falls, added: 'Space is wanting to give a full list of the wounded.' No wonder the Countess murmured to herself every time she saw Elizabeth drive off to the meet: 'God grant that my beloved Empress return whole and sound.'

The Empress, however, could just then bask in the delight of one who has survived a fast hunt over a difficult country where many have not. The experience gained the previous season, too, would have enabled her to appreciate the skill with which she had been piloted across a country which was strange and fences that were formidable. That evening saw the first of the many dinner parties at Cottesbrooke at which she entertained her close friends. Middleton was there, of course, and Spencer (Lady Spencer was wintering at Cannes with the children), Rudi Liechtenstein and Georg and Marie Larisch.

The following day being a Sunday there was no hunting. Rudolph therefore chose it to pay a visit to Cottesbrooke, his only one save at the very end of the stay. Having done so he did not much care for what he saw. Despite his liberal leanings Rudolph had more than his fair share of Habsburg arrogance and self-aloofness. It seemed to him that things were being run on far too free and easy a basis at his mother's country residence. His liking for Middleton can scarcely have been increased by the way his name constantly cropped up in the Empress's conversation. He had, however, a request to make to her on behalf of her cousin the King of Bavaria and, this matter satisfactorily concluded, he returned as quickly as he could to London. There he wrote to Ludwig:

> London, Claridge's Hotel — January 1878
>
> Your Majesty,
>
> My dearest Cousin,
>
> Your Majesty's gracious letter has made me extremely happy . . . I could not reply earlier as until now I have had no opportunity of talking to Mamma by herself. During the journey she was not very well and kept in her

compartment and did not appear at meals which she took with her retinue. Here in London I saw still less of her alone, as her brief stay here was almost entirely taken up with Aunt Marie of Naples and Marie Larisch. I managed to drive over one day to Kotebrook (*sic*) Park, where Mamma is staying. I immediately asked her if she agreed to your plan to accompany her . . . You are so very gracious to inquire about the books which have influenced my religion.'

There was another, also, who did not approve of what he conceived to be his Empress's goings-on with Middleton. Georg Larisch may or may not have been the fool he is said to have been but he, too, had his share of Central-European aristocratic arrogance. 'That fellow Middleton', a mere retired Captain without title or any quarterings whatsoever, was being far too familiar with both the Empress and his wife. Marie Larisch explained to him, with considerable disingenuousness, that the Emperor had totally accepted Middleton at Gödollo and if the All Highest did this who was her husband to object? Mollified by this and a horseman himself as were all his family, he further came round to a more favourable view of Middleton when he saw him schooling one of the Empress's young horses. 'That Englishman may be as mad as a March hare', he told his wife, 'but he knows how to handle a horse.' All the same he remained a disruptive element in the household and both Marie and her Imperial Majesty were pleased and relieved when he announced his intention of finishing the hunting season from Melton.

Then began what should have been, and in many ways was, the happiest period of the Empress's life. Like most shy and complicated people she was really only at home in a small circle; in addition, as with many possessing these traits, she liked to have natural, uncomplicated people about her. She also basked in masculine worship. There she had all of these things. Then, too, she was doing what above all she wanted to do in the presence and company of one who did it better than anyone else. Highly-strung and super-sensitive, the call of action subdued fear and fulfilled something within her. We are not told if she suffered from nerves before hunting but it would seem safe to assume from her temperament that she did. If so, it is entirely in character that they vanished once a fox was away and she caught hold of her horse's head to set him alight after the racing hounds. When hounds ran, she was superb. Of course, she hunted to ride, as did her pilot, for neither of them had much interest in how hounds worked. 'Be with them I will' was the hunting creed both of them lived by. All they asked was a screaming scent and that hounds should run fast and far.

Most of her fellows in the Pytchley field of those days felt much the same. It was a galloping country and those who rode their high-bred and costly horses across it did not come to look at hounds' work. They came for the pace and excitement, the thrill of placing their horses right at the big, stiff fences, surmounting them successfully and galloping on. To the English hunting man and woman of the grass countries in those days three qualities stood supreme: courage, skill and physical beauty. She had them all in abundance. 'A more truly bold and at the same time really graceful rider to hounds has never been seen,' wrote the hunting reporter of *Baily's Magazine* after watching her progress across a country with astonishment and admiration.

It was, when all is said and done, a wonderful achievement for a foreigner, a woman in her forty-first year coming from a country where there was little jumping, to be able not only to hold her own with the regulars but to out-ride them. And they loved her for it, or at least the male members of the field did. Many of her own sex made fun of the fan which was produced from force of habit the moment hounds checked; they said, too, that she owed her place to her pilot which was unfair, for she soon showed that when Middleton had a fall—and he had several, for he could never resist hunting his young horses and riding them as if they were veterans with several seasons behind them—she was quite capable of taking her own line. It must be said, however, that on these occasions, when a problem confronted her, she would look about her for his assistance. Then, almost magically it seemed, fall or no fall, he would be there at her side to help her with his unfailing instinct for the way a fox had gone and the turn and drive of hounds.

She was, indeed, just then, the queen of hearts. She loved it and it brought out the best in her. She was gay and happy and when she was happy she was kind, thoughtful and generous, utterly unlike the selfish, withdrawn, moody creature of Viennese high society. What could be more natural than that she should give most of her attention and affection to the man who was making all this possible for her? 'Bay?' she would call as she had done two years before; 'Bay, where is Bay?' The answer was that Bay was everywhere—hunting, racing, dining, Bay was there and her eyes followed him wherever he went.

The next week he piloted her successfully through a fast hunt from Findon Poplars and she was up to see fox and hounds jump together into the River Nene, the pack making their kill in the water. She was there, too, when the famous black Hemploe fox was killed in the open near North Kilworth House. Soon they began to make expeditions further afield. One was to Mr Tailby's Hounds at Burton Overy. Then they went together to the famous Warwickshire meet at Shuckburgh Hill.

By now she had established a routine for her hunting mornings. If a meet was at or near a private house, and almost all were in those days, a room in it was by arrangement set apart for her. Early in the morning a carriage would drive up to it carrying a 'dresser', usually Frau von Feyfalik, and a footman carrying Her Majesty's carefully packed hunting clothes and other accoutrements which included Her Majesty's personal chamber pot, made of gold and bearing the Imperial arms. A little later, still long before the meet, she would leave Cottesbrooke in a single horse brougham with an equerry in attendance. Before she set out she would have taken a bowl of soup, a special mixture of her own consisting of game, beef and chicken boiled together, and nothing else. This would constitute her entire nourishment for the day. Calling once at the house of Mr Nethercote, one of the historians of the Pytchley, after the day was over, she smilingly rejected the offer of tea and instead asked for a glass of beer which she drank with relish.

When she arrived in the brougham at the chosen house she would be wearing walking dress. At the entrance the owners met her and escorted her to the room made ready for her. Then would come the business of dressing for the chase. With the assistance of the dresser she was sewn first into the chamois undergarment and then into her habit. She had brought no less than sixteen habits with her and others were ordered from

London during her stay. When she was satisfied—and this often necessitated changes of habit and much stitching and unstitching—and not before, she made her appearance. In this respect the Empress had a truly regal disregard for the convenience of others and moving off was frequently delayed.

When this behaviour caused upset and annoyance to himself, his hounds and his field, not every Master was prepared to be as tolerant as Spencer. The Shuckburgh day was a case in point.

The Empress and Middleton arrived no less than an hour late. The Master of the Warwickshire was then Lord Willoughby de Broke, one of the most famous Masters of Foxhounds of his day, and he was not best pleased at thus being kept waiting. When the appointed time passed and she did not come he began to send out picquets in various directions to ascertain her whereabouts and to apprise him of when he could expect her. Meanwhile he fulminated in silence to the growing apprehension of his field.

The Victorians had a passion for recording events such as this in light verse. One such versifier was present then and he set it all down as he saw it:

Who is this that rides down, all importance and hurry?
From his figure and face, I should say 'tis George Currey.
'The Empress is comin'.' He passes the word.
With varying emotion each bosom is stirred.
But all that the Master says—speaking to 'Will'—
Is 'Bid Orvis draw Calcott—then Shuckburgh Hill.'

And as she joined them the chronicler did not omit to record his impressions of the Empress and her companion:

'The bright star of Europe' her kingdom has left,
And Austria mourns of its Empress bereft.
Firm seat in the saddle: light hands on the reins,
As e'er guided steed over Hungary's plains:
She has come—with her beauty, grace, courage and skill
To ride, with our hounds, from old Shuckburgh Hill.

The Captain rides up—as her escort and knight—
To guide her in safey from morning till night;
And those who chose for her have chosen aright.
No braver, no better, no quicker to hounds,

Ever crossed the wide pastures—the far stretching 'grounds'
That reach from the confines of Melton until
They rise from the summit of Shuckburgh Hill.

And then, when they got there:

There's a whimper, a challenge, a chorus, a cheer;
'Tis a Lombard Street bank to a pawnbroker's till,
That a fox is afoot on old Shuckburgh Hill.

A fox was indeed afoot and they were rewarded then with a fast and flying hunt. The bruising manner in which they rode it did not, however, commend itself to Lord Willoughby de Broke who was not prepared to extend to them the same latitude in the matter of riding on top of hounds as did Spencer. 'The huntsman was nowhere about, nor did I see anything more of the whips. The Master, too, a very disagreeable man, was more behind me than in front of me,' the Empress wrote of that day to the Emperor. It was not exactly the sort of behaviour likely to commend itself to one who kept his field in a grip of iron.

When hounds turned for home Middleton rode up to the Master to thank him on behalf of the Empress for the sport he had shown her and to make his amends. Willoughby de Broke turned on him. 'Damn you, Bay', he said, 'You arrived an hour late and you've ridden over my hounds all day.'

Standing nearby the Empress heard the exchange. She immediately moved over to the Master. Laying her hand on his arm and looking up into his eyes she said: 'But you will forgive him for my sake.'

It was an utterly charming and spontaneous gesture and of course it was successful. But the many bystanders all about, dismounting, giving their hunters to grooms, getting their carriages or hacks, or doing the hundred and one things that are done at the end of a hunt, saw it and heard it too.

It and other similar little instances could not but give rise to gossip and every hunting community is a hotbed of gossip. Moreover, it began to be noticed that on occasions when piloting her Bay was acting out of character. He who was always in front was now sometimes, when the fences were tall and thick, quite out of the first flight. After a hunt in a country fenced with more bullfinches than usual she wrote to the Emperor that Bay had had 'a terribly prudent day', and described how—mindful surely of the injunction that she should not scratch her face—he had dismounted and had on foot broken a hole in a fence for her to jump through.

It did not escape attention either that, as their intimacy grew, his language to her became rougher as he shouted to her not to take a turn or to avoid a bad place in a fence. She obeyed him meekly for she knew she was in the presence of a master of his art, that alone amongst women she was privileged in having his skills demonstrated for her pleasure and benefit. She looked beautiful and rode like an angel. Under her light hands and firm seat, and with his genius to guide her, the big, blood horses he had bought for her galloped and jumped her into hunting immortality.

To add to her pleasure there were the evening parties at Cottesbrooke and Althorp and other carefully selected country houses, attended only by her close friends. She was entirely happy for that short time and she looked it. She was vibrant, glowing and entranced. At the same time there was something regal and untouchable about her. Her circle raved about her beauty, naturalness and charm and compared her to the picture of Gainsborough's 'White Lady' which hung in the hall at Cottesbrooke. Even Franz Joseph was now included in her happiness. 'If only you were here! I say it every day I hunt, and how popular you would be for your riding and the way you understand hunting . . . I thought of you so much. If only we could share and share alike . . . I am always telling Lord Spencer how much you would enjoy it. I like him very much, he is so nice and natural, and I think if ever he pays you a visit you will like him, too.'

It is probable, in fact, that the last thing she wanted just then was a visit from the Emperor, for even when they were at Gödollo their paths seldom crossed. But when she was happy her happiness overflowed and she had to communicate it. These messages were more an expression of her mood than a sincere wish to have her husband at her side. It was this euphoria derived from health and action as well as her gratitude to him and affection for him and enjoyment of his company which made her insist on having Middleton always with her whether in the saddle or out of it. He was present at all the Cottesbrooke

Above left Elizabeth in 1852, aged 15 (lithograph by H. Kohler)

Above right Franz Joseph at the time of his marriage

Left Elizabeth at the time of her betrothal

Elizabeth on the circus horse Avolo in 1876

Marie Festetics and Ida Frenczy mounted on the Khedive's donkeys during a visit to Egypt

Elizabeth using a leather fan to conceal her face from onlookers at a meet in Hungary

Left The fifth Earl Spencer (cartoon from *Vanity Fair*). *Right* The Hohenembs Cup. The inscription reads 'The Pytchley Hunt Steeplechases 1878. Won by Captain Middleton's Piccadilly. 6 years. 8 ran.' *Below* Easton Neston

Elizabeth (by C. de Grimm for *Vanity Fair*)

Bay Middleton (from *Vanity Fair* 1883)

Left Marie Larisch with one of the Empress's circus horses, in the garden at Gödollo. *Right* Crown Prince Rudolph, aged 20. *Below* Cottesbrooke

Summerhill

Bay Middleton

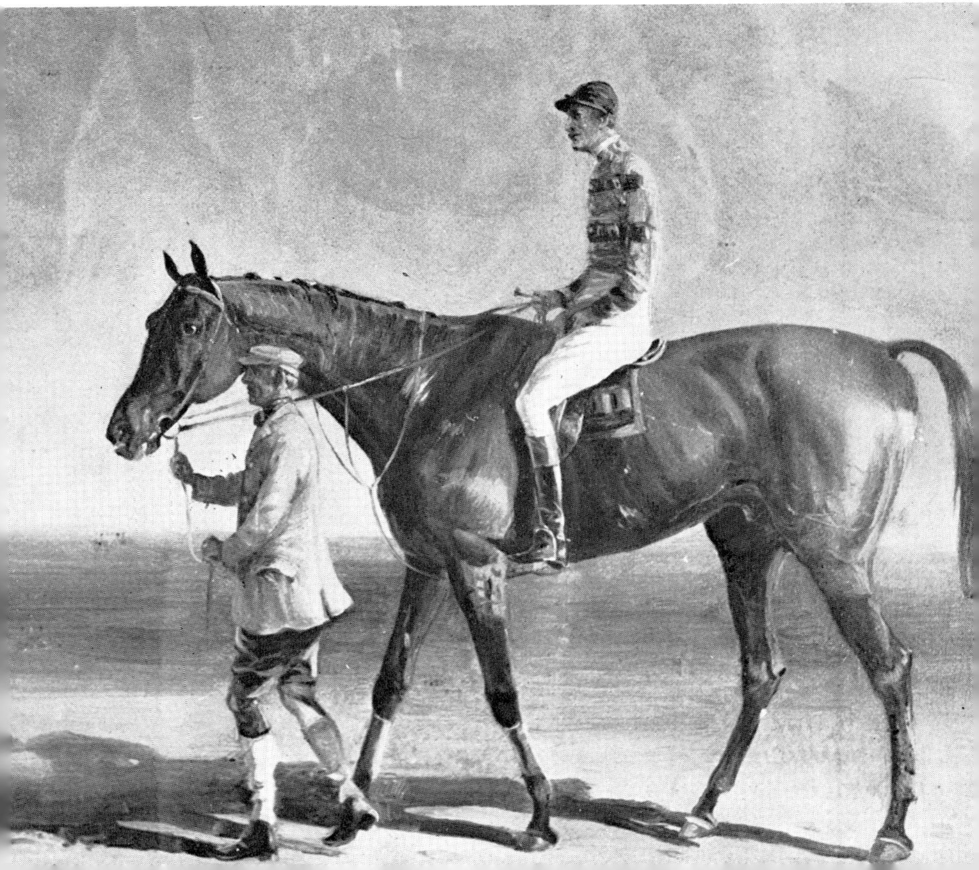

Left Elizabeth hunting with the Meath Hounds, April 1879. *Right* Count Charles Kinsky. *Below* Bay Middleton on Doneraile (by Basil Nightingale, 1895)

and Althorp parties and went with her on the few expeditions she made when she was not hunting.

She thought she had succeeded in shutting out the world and, for the moment, she had. It does not seem to have occurred to her that there is a serpent in every Eden. Nor does it appear to have crossed her mind that her very conduct in restricting her company to only a few must arouse resentment in those who were excluded from the charmed circle.

Grave offence, too, was taken in Vienna when the news was carried back that she was entertaining a Mr Jacques Schawell at Cottesbrooke and had even had him to stay the night despite the limited accommodation in the house. Schawell was the leading horse-dealer in Vienna. He imported hunters and hacks from England and Ireland, sold them to the aristocracy and supplied horses to the Imperial court. Before the advent of Middleton and her English friends he had advised the Empress on her purchases and had bought and sold horses for her. A very fine-looking man, always beautifully dressed and a magnificent horseman, he drove one of the smartest outfits in the Prater. He was a frequent visitor to the Shires to hunt and to buy for his stable and was almost as well-known there as in Vienna. But he could never have dreamt of being received in the Hofburg, and the fact that the Empress was entertaining him at her English residence caused Viennese eyebrows to be raised higher than ever, and indeed some of the stricter members of English society also disapproved of it.

With her position, ability, looks and dash, the eyes of everyone were upon her and the world would not stay shut out. However hard she tried she was not a private person and could never become one. To the end of her days this inability to escape haunted her and brought tragedy to her.

It was the Queen of Naples who acted as the catalyst in causing mischief and bringing unhappiness to her sister. She had neither forgotten nor forgiven Middleton's refusal to pilot her the previous season nor the words in which the refusal had been uttered. She also felt herself cast into the shade by the beauty and abilities of the Empress. Elizabeth was now, through the horse-coping ability of the hated Middleton, far better mounted than the Queen and was attracting the attention her sister felt should have been hers. After all she had come to the

Shires earlier than Elizabeth and had been the means of introducing her sister to the sport. But no one took very much notice of the Queen that season and she was, besides, handicapped by a husband whom almost everyone disliked. The Crown Princess of Prussia writing to Queen Victoria some years before had described him as 'a wretched object . . . too frightful, stammers and twitches with his eyes'. He was indeed a striking contrast to the gallant and glamourous Middleton who had spurned her.

The Queen, of course, was still very much in society and she had a barbed and forked tongue when she wanted to use it. Countess Festetics, scenting danger from that quarter to her beloved mistress, wrote of her in her diary: 'Pointed nose and pointed chin. There sits the devil in between.' The Countess, as usual where Elizabeth's interests were concerned, exaggerated, but that the Queen dropped hints and barbed references about her sister and Middleton where they were likely to do most damage and cause most trouble there can be little doubt. She came up from the Shires and she and her husband lunched with Rudolph privately at Eaton Place late in January just before Rudolph left for Lanarkshire to shoot with the Prince of Wales and the Duke of Hamilton. It seems it was at this luncheon that she conveyed all the hunting gossip to Rudolph and it was there that the mischief was made.

Rudolph's tour was being a great success. He had inherited much of his mother's charm when he wanted to use it and Queen Victoria had been greatly taken with him. He had stayed two nights at Osborne and had borne himself admirably during the formal dinners, making himself pleasant to the elderly members of the Queen's court who were summoned to meet him. 'The Queen is in love with the Crown Prince but do not worry she does not want to marry him,' Princess Mary of Cambridge wrote to the Austrian Ambassador. At Hamilton Palace they bagged over a thousand head of game which must have delighted Rudolph who revelled in slaughter and *battues*. The Prince of Wales was in some trouble from the Glasgow Working Men's Protestant Association for travelling to Hamilton Palace on a Sunday but this did not affect Rudolph. He stayed on to attend a banquet given in his honour. After returning to London and paying a visit at his express request to the newly formed Falconry Club in Alexandra Park where he observed with interest and excitement the hawks swooping on and killing pigeons, the serious business of the tour began.

The Crown Prince visited Liverpool, Manchester and Bradford to inspect docks and factories. At Sheffield he saw armour plate being manufactured for the Austrian government and was presented with a hunting knife. He went to Belfast to see the shipyards. After that came a visit to Dublin where he prudently declined the offer of a mount with the Ward Union Staghounds and followed the hunt instead from the safety of a hack car.

During these visits he was quite away from the stultifying and retrograde atmosphere of the Imperial court. He did not confine himself to meeting official dignataries but was in touch with liberal thought and had representatives of all shades of opinion presented to him. He was much taken, too, with English girls and told a sporting friend that they had the Continentals 'quite beat in looks, shape and action'. They, it seems, were also highly appreciative of him, for he danced 'till four in the morning' at two London balls immediately on his return from Ireland. He paid court as well to Lily Langtry, thus discomfiting Moreton Frewen who at that time regarded himself as the man in possession and who had to leave 'inconveniently' on several occasions when the Crown Prince called.

Indeed wherever he went this personable Prince was a great success. All this, combined with the sudden unshackling of Imperial fetters, may well have gone to his head and, together with his aunt's mischief-making, have accounted for his subsequent behaviour to Middleton.

It is not certain at which of the many balls he attended that the incident occurred but it seems likely that it was that given by the German Ambassador at Carlton House Terrace. The Crown Prince had had a busy day. He had received a deputation of prominent Hungarians, visited the Royal Academy, lunched with the Prince and Princess of Wales at Marlborough House and dined at the Turf Club, before going on to the ball. Middleton was also at the ball as were several other members of the sporting set. Middleton and Rudolph had not met during the visit and a friend, in all innocence, presented Middleton to the Crown Prince. With every inch of Habsburg hauteur alive in his expression and gesture Rudolph drew himself up and stared at the other man in cold silence. Then he turned on his heel and walked away.

It was a flagrant insult given in the most public and damaging circumstances. Rudolph was fortunate indeed that he was his mother's son. Had the circumstances been different, Middleton would not have suffered such conduct meekly from anyone however highly he had been born. If he had been other than who he was His Imperial Highness the Crown Prince of Austria would almost certainly have carried the marks of the hardest man in England with him to his grave. As it was, thanks to Middleton's restraint, the encounter passed without further incident but it did not escape notice which was, no doubt, exactly what Rudolph had intended. News of it went round the ballroom like wildfire; next morning it was in the drawing rooms and from thence it was carried to the hunting countries.

It was, of course, inevitable that the Empress should hear of it. Again it was probably Rudolph's intention that his disapproval of his mother's conduct should be brought to her notice. When the news was carried to her she was both deeply hurt and coldly furious. After the manner of natures such as hers, she imagined that everyone was looking at her, talking about her and pointing the finger of scorn at her. The charmed and happy atmosphere she had built up about her so successfully was shattered. Now all was disenchantment and disillusion. When she went hunting the fan was more in evidence than ever to shield her from the scornful glances of the other members of the field most of which existed only in her imagination. Her first reaction indeed, as usual on occasions such as these, was to cut and run.

An abandonment of the visit and an immediate return to Austria was uppermost in her mind when she recalled or was reminded that she had asked Bay and Captain Soames to organise Pytchley Hunt Steeplechases to be run for in a week's time. These were to be held at her special request and to be financed entirely by her. She had promised to present two cups, one for subscribers with conditions similar to those for her cup two years earlier and one for farmers. Even she, in her present state of mind, could scarcely contemplate cancelling these. Since Bay was so closely concerned, it would almost amount to an act of renunciation. In addition, although this was likely to have carried less weight with her, the Spencers were entertaining the Princess of Wales for the occasion and she had promised to give a banquet at Cottesbrooke for their illustrious guest the evening before racing.

A formal announcement was made that the tour would end on the day of the point-to-point and that she would leave for the continent immediately after the last race. Then she took to her bed. She was suffering from some sort of nervous reaction but she let it be known outside Cottesbrooke that she was mourning Pope Pius IX who had just died. 'Since I am not hunting people will say it is on account of the Pope. So it is most opportune.'

That it was Rudolph who had caused all this unhappiness wounded her more seriously than anything else. He was her son whom she had rescued from Gondrecourt and whom she had caused to be brought on this tour thus giving him the opportunity to enjoy a fuller life and develop his talents and character. She never forgave him. Relations between mother and son steadily worsened thereafter until they virtually ceased to communicate at all and thus yet another step was taken on the road to Mayerling.

She roused herself, however, to attend a last meet at Hannington the day before the races. Word had got round that she would be out again and there was a tremendous turn-out of the swells. Practically her whole suite came with her: Rudi Liechtenstein, of course; all the Larischs, Prince Kinsky and Count Clam-Gallas, by this time quite recovered from his fall. Even Countess Festetics, who loathed hunting, came in a carriage. The Princess of Wales drove over from Althorp with Lady Spencer, now returned from Cannes. Princess Mary of Cambridge, the Duke of Teck, even the ex-King of Naples were also there, to say nothing of a host of hard-riding celebrities from neighbouring hunts. Captain Middleton acted as her pilot, put her into the saddle and they rode together to the first draw.

However fitting it would be to record that they were all rewarded with a red-letter day it would not be true. It was a poor, patchy, bad-scenting day and, mindful of the banquet that evening, Spencer took hounds home early in the afternoon.

It was a tribute to her feeling of friendship for the Spencers that the Empress had undertaken to give for them the sort of formal entertainment that she hated and, moreover, that she went through with it. Worse still from her point of view, it had appeared proper that Rudolph should be asked. He had accepted and he attended bringing Bombelles with him. It is significant, in view of Rudolph's presence, that the name of Captain Middleton, who had been at her side throughout the visit, does not appear amongst the list of guests. Someone, whether Middleton or herself, had the sense not to risk a repetition of the earlier incident.

No one knows what passed between mother and son during the evening but Rudolph stayed the night and went racing with the Imperial party the following day. The Empress, indeed, may not have had much time for any social exchanges with her son. Dressing for the banquet would have started almost as soon as she returned from hunting and the following morning she is said to have risen early to go over to the point-to-point course. There, with Rudi Liechtenstein, she schooled over some of the fences in order to see what riding in an English point-to-point was like. Then she had to change again in order to receive her luncheon guests on the course.

A tremendous show had been put on in her honour by Bay and Soames. Two pavilions had been built for the Imperial and Royal party with railed-off enclosures in front of them from which racing could be viewed. One was used as a luncheon room; the other, suitably decorated with flowers, as a drawing room for the ladies.

At the Empress's express desire Goodall was brought up to bid her goodbye. She made a little speech, prettily thanking him for all the splendid sport he had shown her, and then gave him a jewelled token to remember her by. It was one of her nicest characteristics that she never forgot servants. On her previous visit Beers, the Grafton huntsman, had been presented with a stock-pin of twenty-five diamonds surrounding a sapphire.

The Princess of Wales arrived at twelve-forty. Since the first race was a mere affair of farmers and 'those tradesmen who have taken a Pytchley hound puppy at walk during the current season', no one took much notice of it and luncheon was served immediately afterwards. This was a sumptuous spread laid on by Gunter & Co of London, who had also been responsible for the banquet the night before, and ran the whole gamut: *Potages: à la Reine; Julienne. Saumon à la Hollandaise, Poulardes à la*

Financière, Filets de Boeuf à la Jardinière, Salades de Homard, Pâtés de Gibier, Gelées, Chartreuses, Crêmes, Patisserie. The band of the 3rd Northampton Rifle Volunteer Corps played during luncheon and at intervals throughout the afternoon.

Captain Middleton was amongst the gilded throng present at the luncheon though he cannot have stayed very long or partaken of much of it since he was riding in the next race.

This race was the Empress's own, the Hohenembs Cup. There were eight runners and Middleton's grey gelding Piccadilly was a raging favourite at 6–4 against. It was a glorious sunny March day but there had been some considerable rain in the past few days and, as a consequence, the course rode very heavy.

Owing to the short price offered against Piccadilly Moreton Frewen had difficulty in getting anyone to lay him the odds to £25. He was quite sure Middleton was going to win for he had had a dream. Racing dreams are commonplace enough and most of them are both misleading and mistaken, but the circumstances surrounding this one are so out of the ordinary that they bear re-telling.

Frewen was staying for the season in Lord Castlereagh's house-party at Keythorpe. A short time before the race he dreamt he saw Middleton on a grey horse winning the Empress's Cup with no one in the same field as him. At breakfast the next morning he recounted his dream to his fellow guests adding that it was so vivid and clear that it had convinced him and 'we might as well all scratch our horses'.

Arthur Coventry, a leading Gentleman rider, who later became equally celebrated as starter to the Jockey Club, was staying at the house. He looked up from the table and said: 'That can't be right. I have seen Bay's horses recently and there isn't a grey amongst them.'

Frewen, however, was not to be put off. Meeting Middleton out hunting a day or so later he said to him: 'Have you a grey horse you intend to run for the Empress's Cup?'

'Yes,' was the answer, 'I have. I bought a grey from Cat Richardson for the race only the other day.' Frewen then recounted his dream and added: 'You will win.'

'He should win it all right,' Middleton said. 'He's a class horse. But', he added with typical shrewdness, 'I think he might win the Grand National Hunters' or even a big handicap, so it's a very unlikely dream. Why should I let him expose his form by winning with half-a-mile in hand?' This was sound sense since Middleton, as we know, rode for the plunder. If he could win by the shortest possible distance he was assured of getting extended odds when he ran the grey in the higher-class races he intended to pick up.

As it turned out he broke a stirrup leather over the first fence. The horse, a tremendously hard puller, took charge and even Middleton was unable to hold him. They won at their ease with no one else in sight, exactly as Frewen's dream had foretold. To add a further convincing detail Frewen asserted that in his dream Bay's face at the finish was scarlet with exertion and, according to him, this was also so in fact since Bay had fought with his horse all the way round in his efforts to restrain him. At all events the Empress's second cup was safely his.

Bay also won the Pytchley Hunt Cup but not, perhaps, quite in the way he expected. He ran two, Minotaur and Zouave, putting Hugh Owen up on Minotaur and taking the mount on Zouave himself. Lord Spencer's Remorse was made a hot favourite and of Middleton's two Minotaur was the more fancied by the public. Remorse fell at half-way leaving Minotaur, Zouave and Nut Brown, the second favourite, to fight it out. They finished in that order but Hugh Owen could not draw the weight. He was disqualified and the race awarded to Middleton. So he had a double but a most unusual one.

Once more the Empress had the pleasure and delight of presenting her cup to Bay. But the presence of Rudolph, the feeling of scandal and gossip all about her, much of it perhaps only a figment of her imagination, ruined her enjoyment of the occasion. Immediately after racing she departed for Paris and Vienna, leaving Rudolph and his suite to make their own way home a fortnight later. Although one who recorded these events expressed the wish that 'it is sincerely to be hoped that it was not her last day in the Pytchley country where her presence has been a pleasure and pride for the past two months', she herself in her implacable way was resolved never to return to that disenchanted Eden.

CHAPTER SEVEN

Ireland

'Dancing, drink, debts and "divarsion"' was the way in which a sporting Englishman returning to his own country described life amongst the Anglo-Irish gentry in the latter half of the nineteenth century. And of 'divarsions' the greatest and most enthusiastically pursued was fox-hunting. It was, of course, fox-hunting that brought the Empress to Ireland but she arrived at a singularly unhappy time.

Irish country life had altered very little since the previous century. The gentry still enjoyed privilege without responsibility. They chased the fox, squandered their money, dissipated their estates and alternately harassed and exploited their tenants. The gap between the haves and the have-nots was truly enormous, far greater even than in England where the effects of the Industrial Revolution had begun to shake the rigid barriers of class and offer opportunity to the masses. Nothing at all comparable was happening in Ireland.

By the time the year 1879 came round a succession of bad summers had devastated the potato crop in the west and it was to the potato that the peasant and small farmer looked for his sustenance. 'The air was sick with the rotten smell of potato blight' and in that year alone, since the landlords refused to abate or postpone rents and their collection, no fewer than 1,238 families—6,000 persons—were evicted from their homes and left with the alternative of starvation or emigration. In such a situation the tide of agrarian unrest could not but rise. With it rose the power and influence of Parnell, a consummately skilful politician who in that year, 1879, succeeded in fusing all the disparate elements of Irish protest, the relics of the Fenians, the

Parliamentary Party and the Home Rulers, into a combined body dedicated to 'a war against landlordism for a root settlement of the land question'.

Into this seething atmosphere of discontent, unrest and potential violence the Empress and Middleton (political innocents if ever there were any) suddenly arrived in February 1879. That they undertook the expedition at all must lie at the direct responsibility of the one man most likely, one would have expected, to oppose it: the Earl Spencer, the ex-Viceroy.

It seems quite clear that when she left Northamptonshire in March 1878 the Empress had no thought of hunting in Ireland. She was, however, quite determined never to return to the Shires. She had been hurt there and for her one wound was sufficient to blacken a person or a place forever. But Spencer had in no way been connected with that hurt. Her friendship and affection for him remained intact. She had intended that he should be asked to stay with her in Austria and this was duly done. Early that summer he and Lady Spencer arrived at Ischll to make the acquaintance of the Emperor just as she had promised. Spencer appears to have made a good impression on Franz Joseph and to some extent at least to have gained his confidence. But Franz Joseph soon returned to Vienna, his desk and all the cares of State. The Empress moved on to Tegernsee to attend the celebrations of her parents' golden wedding.

Middleton, meanwhile, had been as usual living the hectic life. A week after the Empress's departure for Vienna, he and Moreton Frewen had taken two horses to Towcester to run for a cup presented by the Queen of Naples. The horses were Victor and Merry Andrew, the horse the Empress had hunted two seasons before. Victor, according to Frewen, was a real good thing but he was entered for a big race later on. If he won at Towcester he would incur a penalty for the big race so they decided to give him a gallop with Frewen up while Middleton rode and declared to win with Merry Andrew.

They thought they had the race to themselves and, coming into the straight, were deciding between them by how much Merry Andrew should win when 'a Newmarket cast-off' came from nowhere and did them both, a result incidentally which can scarcely have done other than give extreme gratification to the donor of the cup. Merry Andrew was subsequently tried by

Middleton on the racecourse proper and proved a failure.

Frewen, who was much younger than Middleton and yet another hero-worshipper, blamed himself for this upset to their plans. When he was getting up a party to stay at Naple's Hotel in Kildare Street for the Dublin Horse Show he included Middleton along with Chicken Hartopp in his invitations. Evenings at the Dublin Horse Show, once the business of the day is over, are traditionally given over to prank and frolic which was even wilder then than now. When Frewen arrived with his guest list at the hotel he ran into unexpected difficulties. For Frederick Naple, the proprietor, flatly refused to have Hartopp or Middleton inside his hostelry. 'To have those two captains here at the same time and table—that is just tempting Providence,' he said. 'Everyone this end of Kildare Street will need police protection.'

Frewen pleaded with him but Naple was adamant and it then transpired that only last year, to use Frewen's own words 'It was the Chicken Captain but it might as well have been the other', had thrown the head waiter through the window with the result that he had had to go to hospital with his injuries. After much argument the head waiter himself was summoned and, after listening to Frewen's pleas and promises, agreed to wait on the two 'savage sabreurs' saying 'I'll chance it. They gave me ten pounds anyhow.'

It is clear from this that Middleton's Regency-like reputation had not diminished since his association with the Empress nor had his behaviour mellowed—except when she was there. No mention is anywhere made by her intimates or those associated with her of his behaving in her presence or company or in any of the house parties she graced with anything other than courtier-like correctness. That she thus tamed him is evidence in itself of the bond that existed between them.

By the time the Dublin Horse Show was over another invitation summoned Bay back to Gödollo. The house party there that autumn included Lord and Lady Spencer but the Emperor did not join them. He was still in the Schönbrunn shouldering alone the burden of his terrible responsibilities without confidante or comforter by night or day for Frau Schratt had not yet come on the scene.

At Gödollo the horse reigned supreme. The Empress had two

greys, Flick and Flock, whom she was training herself as circus horses. The party would gather each day to watch her as she put them through their paces in the private riding school she had built in the palace grounds. Then hunting started once more.

Elizabeth did not attempt to conceal her dissatisfaction with Hungarian hunting after what she had seen and done in England. Even the excitement of leading a cavalry charge in front of the regiment of Hussars of which she was colonel-in-chief and going on manoeuvres with them failed to make up for what she thought she was missing.

She expressed her boredom and longing to both Spencer and Middleton and it seems quite clear that it was Spencer who suggested the Irish adventure. Certainly when it took place the public prints in Ireland openly ascribed to him the responsibility for it. Further, they declared their gratitude to him for the honour he had done to their country by arranging the visit of Her Imperial and Most Catholic Majesty, and he never denied it.

By now, of course, in the Empress's eyes any hunting tour would be inconceivable without Middleton and he, naturally enough, seized on the idea and encouraged it, drawing on his own recollections of the wildness, romance and excitement of Irish hunting. But, unlike the Empress and Middleton, Spencer did not lack knowledge either of the feelings of the English royal family towards Ireland or of the political situation there. Indeed while he was helping to organise the Empress's preparations he was at the same time addressing Gladstone, his personal friend and political chief, a twenty-eight page letter on Irish affairs, what he should do and whom he should see were he to pay that country a visit. He must have known very well the surprise, astonishment and shock the arrival of the Empress, who was not only a reigning royal but a Catholic to boot, was going to cause in court, viceregal and political circles. It was true that her presence was to be camouflaged by an incognito but that cloak was to be expected and indeed proved exceedingly thin.

One can only speculate on Spencer's reasons for suggesting this politically ill-advised expedition and moreover in persuading Franz Joseph that it was unlikely to have any adverse effect on relations between the two countries. The solution, it is suggested, lies in the character of Spencer himself.

Although a Whig grandee Spencer had all the instincts of an autocrat. No taint of liberalism was allowed to enter into his personal relationships. Owning as he did virtually half the county, 26,000 acres in all, he regarded himself and was regarded by all save a few of his less sycophantic followers as the King of Northamptonshire. During his Masterships of the Pytchley no one save himself was allowed any say in the management of the hunt and he refused to countenance the appointment of a hunt committee. His first Mastership, undertaken when he was only twenty-nine, was distinguished by the savage manner in which he controlled his field. 'No regiment of Dragoons', remarked H.O. Nethercote, one of the Pytchley historians who had felt the lash of his tongue, 'was kept under stricter discipline than the Pytchley field at the time.'

Later he mellowed slightly and substituted sarcasm for ferocity but this did not endear him to those less favoured than Middleton and his select coterie. When, during his third and least successful Mastership, a committee was eventually formed he accosted one of them saying: 'So you have got your damned committee, have you? Well, understand this: I'll stand no interference from them, or from anyone else, as long as I'm Master.'

He said himself—almost certainly inaccurately—that he had no political ambitions. Once out of office, therefore, he considered himself free to act as a purely private person. His temperament and position were such, too, as to make him believe that he was a law unto himself. In addition he had just given up his second Mastership of the Pytchley and he may have wished for a change of hunting climate. If so, where better than Ireland where he had so much enjoyed hunting and who better to accompany him than the lovely Empress and his great friend, her pilot, Bay Middleton? There can be little doubt, too, that he, like all the others, had fallen under her spell.

But Spencer would have had to have been a far more obtuse man than he was not to have realised the intense embarrassment of the presence of an ex-Viceroy, a reigning consort who was a woman and an empress, together with a man, widely reported, however erroneously, to be her lover, must cause to the present holder of the Lord Lieutenancy. This was none other than the Duke of Marlborough, and he had troubles of his own.

It is said that when his successor, Abercorn, resigned in 1878 Spencer had ideas of being re-appointed to the Lord Lieutenancy despite the fact that he was on the wrong side of the fence politically. If he did have those ambitions they were to be disappointed. Disraeli dearly loved a duke although the dukes available to him just then were thin enough on the ground. The position cost its holder at least £40,000 a year to fill though the emoluments for it came to only about £20,000, so that besides being a duke the appointee had to have an ample purse.

Disraeli wanted the Duke of Marlborough, and he wrote to the Queen:

> Lord Brownlow will not go; Lord Bradford will not go; Lord Beauchamp, who might have done (though he wd have been a quarrelsome Viceroy) has now lost his wife a necessary appendage for such a post.
>
> Tho' the Duke of Marlboro' is not rich for a Duke he is rich enough for the office. Of late the Duke has been parting with his outlying properties (notably in Bucks where he sold the Waddesdon Estate last year to Ferdinand de Rothschild for £240,000) and has been putting his house in order . . .

Marlborough had already refused the position in 1874. Now he was ready enough to accept but not for the usual reasons. The Aylesford scandal had just broken. The Marquess of Blandford, Marlborough's eldest son, had been or was said to have been about to elope with 'Sporting Joe' Aylesford's wife, when that nobleman was away with the Prince of Wales in India. Sporting Joe, who was no model of propriety or male fidelity himself, made known his intention of instituting divorce proceedings, citing Blandford. Lord Randolph Churchill, Blandford's younger brother, believed or persuaded himself that the Prince of Wales was behind Sporting Joe's actions. He obtained possession of letters written by the Prince to Lady Blandford and threatened to publish them unless proceedings were dropped. A furious row blew up culminating in a challenge to a duel issued by the Prince to Churchill. Finally proceedings, duel and undue publicity were all averted by the belated exercise of commonsense. But the Prince was not mollified and issued a ukase virtually banning the whole Churchill family from Society.

Marlborough, therefore, despite the cost to his purse, was glad enough to get away from England and the social thunderbolts which the Prince was hurling at him. Lord Randolph Churchill and his newly married wife, the famous Jennie Jerome, one of the reigning beauties of her day and any day, went with him, Churchill as his private secretary.

It was, of course, virtual exile and was seen as such by Society. Marlborough, who himself had no hand in the whole unseemly affair but who had remained loyal to his son, was anxious enough to earn remission of his banishment and to return to royal favour, nor did he desire to do anything which would further offend court circles. Now he was confronted with this delicate situation created by a foreign Catholic monarch paying a visit to his unsettled domains under an incognito that looked to be no incognito at all and around whom, however innocent she herself might be, the forces of disaffection were almost certain to give at least the pretence of rallying.

None of these things would have had any effect on the Empress had she either known or thought of them at all, which is unlikely. They should, however, have carried weight with Franz Joseph if he had considered them. This he almost certainly must have done for, whatever his faults, he was a most experienced and conscientious monarch. By now he must have known enough of the power and resources of the English nation and the formidable character of its Queen not to risk causing offence to either of them in an area where they were vulnerable—the governing of the unruly Irish. Moreover he had an especial reason for being sympathetic to them in their troubles with that country for he himself had had on his hands a very similar situation in Hungary. Indeed Queen Victoria had already compared the Imperial difficulties in Hungary with those of her own in Ireland. One can only assume that, beset on all sides with the vast cares of his huge Empire, in discussing the matter with Spencer he was content to take the advice of an ex-Viceroy whom he was entitled to treat as an expert on the subject, and to abide by it.

At all events the preparations went ahead though at the outset they were a well kept secret. The first thing, of course, was to secure a suitable residence for Her Imperial Majesty. Here again the knowledge Spencer and Middleton had gained and the friendships they had formed in Ireland and the Shires came in useful.

Meath, 'Royal' Meath, hunted by the smartest pack in Ireland was, of course, the chosen county. And in Meath the fourth Lord Langford, 'Paddy' Langford to his friends and a crony of Spencer and Middleton, had a splendid and centrally situated mansion at Summerhill. To make matters easier Langford himself, though he held the sinecure position of State Steward of Ireland, was seldom in residence at his Irish seat. During the winter he hunted from Melton and in summer he was often abroad. Linger arranged all the details which included the fact that Langford was to be allowed to join the Imperial party and to stay in his own house as a guest of the Empress. Jacques Schawell was also brought over to advise and help with the horses and stayed in Summerhill as a member of the household. The question of horses was a difficult one for none of the Empress's horses had any experience of jumping Irish banks. She had left nine of them behind her in Northamptonshire the year before. These were sent over to Ireland to be schooled and made ready for her by Edward MacDonald, who had been taken on as stud-groom, and Tom Healy who was engaged as a rough rider. Middleton, too, paid frequent visits to Ireland to supervise the schooling and the stud. The Empress's horses were, however, used to jumping fast from a gallop and were also accustomed to a side-saddle and her feather-weight on their backs. They did not take kindly to the strong handling of the two men nor to the stopping and propping necessary for safe bank jumping and three of them were killed during this schooling process. To fill the gap in the stud at least to some extent Middleton sold her the failed steeplechaser Merry Andrew. At first sight an ex-steeplechaser does not look to have been a very wise choice or safe conveyance for a lady over an Irish country, but in fact Middleton schooled him for her himself and before the Irish visit was well advanced she was riding him and going superbly on him. Middleton really had something approaching genius in matching mount and rider where she was concerned.

She was desolate when she heard of the accidents to her beloved horses. There were other worries too, for a fortnight before Christmas Rudolph shot himself in the hand with a sporting rifle. Rudolph really was quite an appalling muff where field sports were concerned. A little later he succeeded in shooting and killing a beater. The wretched man's family were bought off with a payment of fifty gulden, a trifling solatium indeed from the scion of the richest reigning family in the world. This incident moved one writer hostile to the regime to comment that whenever a member of the Habsburgs shot a beater or a guest at a shooting party, or insulted anyone, or gave anyone a venereal disease, he behaved as though the victim had been honoured. And Countess Festetics, ever ready with her pen, recorded in her diary after the first incident: 'Every creature that breathes or has wings is doomed to death. Some men become possessed of a sort of lust for killing.' In fact Rudolph's visit to England, though it may have broadened his outlook, had removed almost all the vestiges of self-discipline that remained in his character and he was very firmly banned from joining the suite that was being assembled for Ireland.

This was small and select indeed. Georg and Marie Larisch had retired into mutual disharmony in the Hotel Imperial on the Ringstrasse in Vienna. Here Marie was at first left alone much of the time and she spent it getting up to mischief with the Baltazzis and others. Her husband was house-hunting for a suitable residence near the family estates at Solza. Finally he found one at Friestat and to this they moved early in 1879 away from the Empress and her circle.

Apart from Spencer and Middleton, Rudi Liechtenstein and Heinrich Larisch were the only close friends who accompanied her. Nopsca, of course, came along as head of her household, Countess Festetics as lady-in-waiting and Langyi as her physician.

By February the secret was out and the visit made official or, rather, semi-official, since it was to be conducted under the Empress's favourite incognito of the Countess Hohenembs. Count Karolyi, the Austrian Ambassador who had succeeded Beust, called on the Duke of Connaught on 12 February to break the news to him. The Duke immediately wrote to the Queen conveying it, in turn, to her.

Queen Victoria can scarcely have been gratified to hear of it. Many years before as a young woman the Queen had shown some sympathy for the Irish tenants and their plight. She had also come to some realisation of the dangers inherent in the intense religious differences that wracked the country. As a result she had supported financial aid to the Catholic seminary at Maynooth on the grounds that an educated priesthood must lead to a better understanding between the two countries. Her hopes, pinned on the good results expected to spring from the education of the priesthood were, of course, soon shattered and altogether her romantic attachment to Ireland and the Irish did not last long. At the height of the famine, she displayed neither sympathy nor understanding though in this she was not alone for neither did her ministers or advisers.

Events as a whole combined to further her distrust and dislike for her other island. When the Prince Consort had died she presented a statue of him to the city of Dublin. The Mayor and Corporation refused to accept it and sent it back. This insult to the dearest dead wounded her so gravely that she was reported as saying she would never forgive Ireland. By 1879 her disillusion with the Irish nation and people was total.

The Queen solved the problem of whether or not to make any gesture of recognition to her unwelcome guest by being much preoccupied with preparations for the approaching wedding of the Duke of Connaught. In any event, Karolyi during his interview with the Duke of Connaught had told him that the Empress did not wish to break her journey either in London or Dublin. Thus no official reception or recognition of any sort were accorded the Empress on her arrival. At Dover she was met only by Count and Countess Karolyi and lunched privately with them in the Lord Warden hotel. When the Imperial train reached Holyhead the station doors were locked and all approaches guarded by police to prevent any spontaneous demonstration of welcome. From the station the Empress boarded a specially chartered screw steamer, the *Shamrock*, which brought her safely through heavy snow and fog to Ireland.

At Dublin, although there was no representative of the Lord Lieutenant's staff on the platform, the reception was very different. The Lord Mayor and his attendants together with the Directors and representatives of the railway company were waiting for her there to give her at least a semi-official welcome. Before she boarded the special train which was to take her to Kilcock, the station for Summerhill, she was presented with a bouquet and 'a copy of the time-table, printed on satin, delicately perfumed'.

A huge and enthusiastic crowd witnessed her departure. Along the entire distance of her route the railway was lined with throngs of country people cheering her on her way. At Kilcock a red carpet had been laid down to lead her to her carriage. The Austrian flag flew from the station flag-pole; on the footbridge was a green flag bearing a gold harp and the inscription 'Erin cordially welcomes the Empress'. Outside the station, spanning the crimson carpet, was a triumphal arch of evergreens with worked into them the Irish traditional welcome: '*Céad Mile Fáilthe*' (a hundred thousand welcomes). No English emblem was anywhere to be seen.

Snow was lying thick on the ground as she drove to Summerhill but this did not prevent thousands of country people lining the road to wave and cheer her. At the boundary between Kildare and Meath another triumphal arch had been built, this time bearing the words: 'Welcome to Royal Meath'. Altogether there was precious little that was either private or incognito about Her Majesty's arrival in Ireland.

On the Empress's instructions an immense amount of money had been spent on Summerhill to make it suitable for the accommodation of herself and her suite. A room had been converted into a private Catholic chapel, suitably decorated. A telegraph, too, had been installed with a private line to the continent to obviate the necessity of messages being routed through England, which cannot have pleased either the Queen or the Viceregal court. Indeed the Duke and Duchess of Marlborough made quite clear throughout the visit their embarrassment at the presence amongst them of this Imperial guest who put on and off her incognito as and when it suited her. The Duchess, especially, was in an invidious position socially for she never quite knew who was taking precedence and when. She did not care for her rank as first lady being usurped and her social thunder stolen and she made her disapproval explicit in as many ways as she could.

All this can scarcely have crossed the Empress's mind for she was happy again at the prospect of action and excitement and the renewal of old acquaintances. Spencer and Middleton were waiting for her at Summerhill together with Langford whom they presented to her. The association with Middleton was now gaining something in the nature of semi-official recognition for on her arrival it was announced: 'Captain Middleton will attend her Majesty in the hunting field, but from the thick coating of snow that lay on the ground on Saturday it may be expected that for a day or two at least his services will not be brought into recognition.'

After luncheon she repaired to her apartments and dashed off a letter to Queen Victoria. In its mixture of tactlessness and the all too obvious hasty fulfilling of a boring obligation it is a communication typical of Elizabeth and it is worth quoting in full:

> Countess of Hohenembs to HM the Queen
>
> Summerhill Windsor Castle
>
> 22 February 1879
>
> I am using the first day of my stay in Ireland to announce to Your Majesty my arrival and my intention to keep to the strictest incognito while attempting to acquaint myself with the peculiarities of Irish hunting customs. In respectful consideration of the great sorrow which has befallen the loving motherly heart of Your Majesty I did not wish to disturb with a visit, and pressed by time, have been obliged to hurry on to my destination.
>
> The Emperor asked me to transmit to Your Majesty his devoted greetings, Rudolph kisses hands and gratefully remembers the signal cordiality and courtesy he has received from Your Majesty and I finally would like to recommend myself warmly to Your Majesty's enduring feelings of sisterly affection.

The offhand nature of the contents of this letter was scarcely likely to allay any of the grave misgivings Queen Victoria already had concerning the visit. Its possible effect on her and the consequences that might flow from it were unlikely, however, to have caused the Empress any concern especially since, the following morning, the sun was shining brightly and the snow had gone.

Ireland being a Catholic country Sunday observance was neither as strict nor as stultifying as across the Channel. Once Mass was over no religious sanctions prevented the enjoyment of sporting pursuits. After luncheon that Sunday Middleton and the Empress rode out together.

The next day Elizabeth was due to hunt with the Ward Union Staghounds. She had never in her life seen an Irish bank, much less jumped one. The object of this afternoon's ride was to give her experience in jumping a bank and to allow her to get the feel of a horse over these strange and, to the unaccustomed eye, often fearsome obstacles.

The Meath country (over which the staghounds also hunt) is fenced largely with big, solid banks and wide, deep, open ditches. It should perhaps be explained that jumping a bank is a very different matter from the point of view of both horse and rider from jumping an English fence. In an English grass country the horse jumps big out of his stride, the leap being accomplished and the fence surmounted in one single effort so to speak. In Ireland, when confronted with a bank, the horse must be made to take the obstacle slowly and off his hocks. He jumps on to the top of the bank, pauses there for a second, changes his legs and then jumps out on the other side far enough, his rider hopes, to clear any ditch or other danger which may lurk there. The wide open ditches, too, with their yawning irregular sides are also jumped slowly, and seldom taken at speed.

The enclosures in Meath, though big by Irish standards, are smaller than those in the Shires and banks constitute a more serious impediment to the pace of hounds than the timber and cut-and-laid fences of an English galloping country. Thus hunts in Ireland are not ridden at the same breakneck pace as in the Shires and falls, too, when they come, are usually much less serious than in England for, since the horse jumps more slowly, the impact with the earth is less severe for the rider who has, too, more time to get clear. Nevertheless, the Ward Hounds, when they ran, went fast enough to present problems of nerve, skill and horsemanship even to the experienced. In fact, Whyte-Melville, the hunting versifier, hit it off pretty well when he wrote:

For a horse may be grassed and his rider be floored,
In a couple of shakes when they start with the Ward.

So if Elizabeth were to ride up to her reputation here and stay in the first flight as she had done everywhere else, it was essential that she should be well mounted. She herself, of course, had no intention of being anywhere other than in the van. Neither had her pilot.

Middleton knew from his own experience of Irish hunting that English horses do not take kindly to switching from fast flying fences to the slower methods required for jumping banks. He had watched the Empress's string being schooled and had seen that they were no exceptions to this rule. In his opinion, with the possible exception of Merry Andrew, they were not going to carry her successfully over an Irish country if ridden the way she liked to ride them. Thinking the matter over he went off to consult Leonard Morrogh who had for many years acted as Master of the Ward on behalf of a committee. Morrogh was, in fact, Master in all but name; he knew more about hunting the Meath and Ward countries than any man living and he had gained for himself the sobriquet 'The Nimrod of Ireland'. He suggested to Middleton that he should put at the disposal of the Empress a brilliant hunter of his called Domino who had carried Mrs Morrogh—also a thruster in her own right—with great success for several seasons.

Domino had been brought to Summerhill before the Empress arrived and it was on Domino that she rode out that afternoon with Middleton and schooled over the banks and ditches of the demesne. Seeing how well he performed Middleton advised the Empress, for the beginning at any rate, to leave everything to the horse, to slip her reins at the fences, give him his head and sit still. This she immediately and meekly consented to do. Where horses and horsemanship were concerned she obeyed him like a biddable child. She knew she was in the presence of the best in the world and she had the sense to appreciate that his talents were being put to use for her pleasure alone. It is safe to say that there was not another woman in the world for whom he would have gone to such lengths or taken such trouble to advise and help.

Domino, described as 'a nice blood-like brown hunter of

good substance whose only demerit is a tail or flag worn slightly crooked', was to prove a fit mount for an Empress and it was through Middleton's thoughtfulness and foresight in obtaining him that she was to owe much of her enjoyment and success that season in Ireland.

It was on Domino that Middleton put her up the following morning outside Parsonstown Manor. She had driven over there in a closed carriage before the meet at Batterstown nearby. As usual she was with her dresser for some considerable time and kept the field waiting in her own inimitable way. When she emerged she was seen to be wearing a brown habit and looking radiant. Then there were presentations conducted by Spencer, appearing, in one watcher's eyes at least, to be 'noticeably stouter than when last we saw him'.

Jem Brindley, the huntsman, was brought up, and Leonard Morrogh. A consummate huntsman and horseman, Morrogh's background was unusual for a Master of Hounds in those days. He was, in fact, a practising solicitor though the amount of time and attention he devoted to his clients' affairs cannot have been very great since he hunted four days a week. In a rather patronising biography of him published a year or two before, *Baily's Magazine* had this to say: 'The subject of our memoir was not educated at Eton, nor did he graduate in the arts of peace at Christ Church Oxon or those of war in Chelsea or Knightsbridge Barracks.' Wherever he was educated, he was a magnificent Master and crossed the country superbly; his wife, who had also an unusual background in being a French-Canadian, was not far behind him. But the fact that he came from the city and yet could beat the county on their own ground aroused jealousy in many of the less successful, notably in a Mr Turbett, also a committee member. This, coupled with the touchy temperament Morrogh undoubtedly had, was to be the cause of a real roaring hunting row a few days later.

Batterstown is only fourteen miles from Dublin by train. News of the Empress's intention to hunt had spread far and wide and an immense field turned out to welcome her. Colonel Forster, the Master of the Horse, 'a delightful good-looking courtier' and Captain Chicken Hartopp, who had remained on as ADC to the new Viceroy, represented Dublin Castle. Hartopp came out hunting accompanied by a large coach. In the coach were a brass band and 'drink unlimited'. After hunting or sometimes between coverts he would entertain his friends to the unlimited drink, at the same time having them serenaded by the band. However, on this occasion, neither the drink nor the band nor Hartopp himself were present at the end of the hunt.

The Ward Union hunt a carted stag. The quarry is brought in a van to the point of enlargement or start of the hunt. He is there set free. The field line up behind giving almost the appearance of a mass of cavalry. Hounds are then laid on the scent. After sufficient start has been given, at a signal from the Master, the field sit down to ride—as hard as they can. Again this start somewhat resembles a cavalry charge. The stag is not killed at the end of each hunt but is recaptured unless, of course, he escapes altogether.

On this occasion the enlargement took place at Dunshaughlin Poor House under the supervision of Mr Turbett. Half the huge field were left on the road and the first few fences further thinned those who got away. But there were four who were neither left nor stopped: the Empress, Middleton, Spencer (riding a horse he had borrowed from a Captain Kearney, one of his former ADCs; he, too knew too much to bring over his English horses) and Leonard Morrogh.

The Empress, as it happened, with the luck that often attended her on sporting occasions, had fallen in for one of the best hunts of the season. She certainly had a stern initiation to Irish hunting for the pace at first was terrific: 'as good as a steeplechase and better than most', according to one who recorded it. The country was a stiff one, too, big banks, doubles and singles alternating with great yawning ditches. Piloted by Middleton who, once he had seen what Domino was capable of, took everything as it came and rode as straight as he did in the Shires, she went brilliantly. Domino, with her featherweight on his back, his head free under the lightest of light hands, never put a foot wrong. Together she and Middleton rode out that great hunt. Twelve miles at racing pace with only one check and over that country thinned the field as if a scythe had gone through it. There were many accomplished riders out that day and many good and bold horses but from a field of over a hundred only the four that have been mentioned saw it all and only they, along with Brindley, the huntsman, were there at the finish. Piloted by the best man to hounds in Europe she may have been; it was still a memorable feat to stay with him in her first day in a strange country on a strange horse in a hunt of that length and pace.

As they reached Maynooth there occurred one of those bizarre incidents that always seemed to associate themselves with her in the hunting field or anywhere else.

Workmen were repairing a breach in the demesne wall of the Catholic seminary, Maynooth College. The hunted stag, weary and nearly beaten, jumped through the breach and dived for refuge into a shrubbery within the walls. Hounds poured over after him and, setting Domino at the gap, the Empress followed. She had not, of course, the slightest idea where she was or what premises she was entering. If she thought at all she must have assumed it was the wall around some landowner's demesne. But Middleton and Spencer, both of whom followed her, would have known very well where they were. Since Elizabeth almost jumped on top of Dr Walsh, the President, who had come out to investigate the commotion, it was exactly the sort of escapade which would have appealed to Middleton's zany sense of the ridiculous.

Explanations rapidly followed and Elizabeth was asked by Dr Walsh to enter the college and take refreshment with him. This she did and he then offered her his 'toga' as a wrap against the cold. The offer was graciously accepted and he had the honour of placing it around her shoulders. After the refreshment had been taken the carriages arrived and she drove home, having captivated Dr Walsh and the senior members of the staff by her charm, as she captivated everyone when she wished to. She also promised to return for another longer visit.

So delighted was Mr Morrogh with the way she had ridden Domino in the hunt and so entranced was he with her personally that as she was entering her carriage he there and then went up to her and asked her to accept the horse as a gift and tribute from him and as an honour to the hunt. She thanked him graciously and Domino was hers. It was a generous and magnificent present and Domino was to carry the Empress successfully for many seasons and in different countries. When he died she had his hooves mounted and sent them to Mr Morrogh as a memorial of his kindness.

A garbled version of the Maynooth affair reached the ears of the English cabinet and court. This, coupled with the Marlboroughs' account of her triumphant welcome and all but regal progress from Dublin to Summerhill, caused considerable consternation.

The west of Ireland was by now in the beginning of the agrarian revolt which was to reach its climax a year or so later. The unrest was spreading rapidly eastwards. Catholic priests were amongst the most active of those who organised and directed the illegal activities. The priests were, of course, far better educated than their flock and this, combined with their cloth and its authority, gave them immense power over the ignorant and superstitious peasantry. This improved education for the priesthood not only failed to fulfil Queen Victoria's ideal of improving relations between the two countries, it had in fact gone a long way towards worsening them. She herself had for some time since recognised the notion as being a piece of youthful folly. She now disliked and feared Irish priests and the priesthood almost above everyone else in her unruly and unsettled dominion. These priests had received their education at Maynooth College where the Empress had been disporting herself, and the Queen and her ministers regarded Maynooth, not inaccurately perhaps, as a hotbed of sedition and subversion.

Worse, from English eyes, was to come, and that almost immediately, for Elizabeth did not delay long in making her formal visit. Six days later, the very next Sunday, she drove over to the college to attend Mass instead of having it said privately for her at Summerhill. This was indiscreet enough in all conscience but, to crown her indiscretions, she brought with her in a single closed brougham only the most chosen of her suite, Countess Festetics, Rudi Liechtenstein and—Bay Middleton. It is indeed a signal indication of the closeness of their relations that she chose him to accompany her on an expedition which by no stretch of the imagination could have had anything to do with horses and hunting. That he, a tough Scotch presbyterian, consented to do so and to go within the walls of the citadel of high popery in Ireland and there actually to attend Mass is evidence in itself of his thraldom and devotion. Spencer, showing some belated good sense, did not accompany the party.

A red carpet was laid down upon which her Majesty could walk unsullied to the chapel. Once she was inside, a priedieu and chair were placed for her within the altar rails. Dr McCabe, Bishop of Gadara and Vicar Capitular of Dublin, had come down especially for the occasion. Just what Middleton's thoughts were during the service have not been recorded; perhaps it is just as well.

After Mass the Imperial party went on a tour of the college. The Empress was at her most regal and charming, with a bow and a smile for all. The students gave her three hearty cheers and were rewarded with a free day. Incognito had certainly gone by the board. It was all much more cosy, intimate and enthusiastic than any greeting ever given to a member of the English royal family who were just then, and quite rightly, being advised to stay out of Ireland.

The public prints, which were almost universally nationalistic, got hold of the occasion and the visit and played them up for all they were worth. Not only was it acutely embarrassing for those in position and power in England but, with Ireland in the melting pot, the whole affair held potential danger. If open rebellion were to break out again, and it was only a few short years since the Fenian threat of this had been with difficulty suppressed, the more apprehensive amongst the ruling few wondered if she might not be made into some sort of figurehead behind which the elements of unrest would combine to demand secession. To make matters worse the authorities had not forgotten that the Irish Special Branch, which had been formed with the express purpose of combating Fenianism, had issued them a warning as a result of information gleaned from an informer. This said that Kossuth, the revolutionary from Hungary, the country she loved and in which she spent most of her time, had promised the men of violence in Ireland every assistance in his power were a rising to take place.

But the English, and indeed almost everyone else, were always considerate of Franz Joseph's feelings. He had the ability, stiff and unbending though he was, to inspire both respect and affection in the chancelleries. Buchanan's attitude, expressed in the letter about the luncheon incident when he said he did not wish to upset the Emperor, is typical of this. Though resentment and apprehension mounted in England concerning the visit, no representations were made as to her recall; that was to come later.

Spencer's attitude remains enigmatic as do many of the actions of this strange man. If his advice was asked, as it may have been, he probably counselled that the press, which he disliked and despised, was blowing up the matter out of all proportion and that the disturbances, such as they were, were confined to the western part of the country. His hatred and contempt for journalists and the press was only equalled by that of Lord Kitchener who was accustomed to address reporters: 'Now then, you scum.' Spencer had tried, unsuccessfully, to ban all newspaper reports of the Pytchley and its doings during his masterships. Since these years coincided with the heyday of the hunting correspondent, graced by perhaps the greatest of them all, Captain Pennell-Elmhirst, later himself to be Master of the Woodland Pytchley, this had not increased his popularity. Also, he was not the man to advise on the abandonment of an expedition he himself had originated. But he was given to sudden changes of mind and course. During his second viceroyalty, for instance, he suddenly and enthusiastically espoused the cause of Home Rule which he had once so sternly opposed, thus earning the execration of his former friends amongst the great landowners and the nobility. It may not be without significance, therefore, that he left Meath on 1 March, the day she paid her visit to Maynooth, thus cutting short his stay and returning to Northamptonshire.

Socially, too, there were repercussions. The inclusion of Captain Middleton amongst the three chosen to accompany her to Maynooth could not but set tongues wagging.

Once more he was always at her side. His advice to her about horseflesh was invaluable. Although it was not the practice in Ireland, nor was it necessary, to have two horses out each day as in the Shires, it was obvious to him that her six hunters, even with the addition of the invaluable Domino, were not going to see her through the season. Accordingly he bought for her from the Ward Kennels an experienced grey mare called The Widow who had for many seasons carried Charlie Brindley, the famous Ward huntsman and father of Jem who had just succeeded him. Other purchases were made locally and very successfully though, as may be imagined, at prices which were long and steep.

It was Middleton, too, and not Nopsca, Spencer, Heinrich Larisch or any of the official suite whom on that very first day Morrogh approached regarding the possibility of a bye-day especially for Her Majesty. Morrogh's idea was that they might hunt an outlier to show the Empress how this was done and have some sport with a small and select field. Unknown to him Mr Turbett made the same approach, also to Middleton, but his was more definite for he had a place in mind and an outlying stag whose whereabouts had been made known to him, in view.

The exact circumstances in which the arrangements for that bye-day were made became the subject of an acrimonious dispute. It is sufficient to mention here that after an unsatisfactory day with the Meath on the Tuesday the Empress and her party turned up to meet Mr Turbett and the Ward Union Hounds at Rathmolyon on the following day, Ash Wednesday; that Mr Turbett, with the permission of the committee, did have some authority for taking hounds out to secure outliers; that he did ask Mr Morrogh's permission on the Monday but that Morrogh understood the permission only extended to Turbett taking Brindley and three couple of hounds to secure the outlier and in no way imagined that a full hunting day was contemplated.

There can be little doubt that Turbett's intention was to steal a march on Morrogh with the Empress and that he succeeded. But his explanations afterwards were both devious and disingenuous. Since Brindley had only permission to bring on three couple of hounds Turbett borrowed two-and-a-half couple from the BDH and another two-and-a-half from Lord Killeen to make up a pack. He also had to admit that the previous day, when with the Meath, he had told Jacques Schawell of his intention and asked him to convey this information to the Empress since his proposed starting point was to be near Summerhill. Later he received a message, as he must have hoped he would, that the Empress would be delighted to join him. He must also have leaked the information to the press for the *Freeman's Journal* reporter, who had been specially assigned to cover the Empress's visit, arrived in a side-car at the meet.

The whole Summerhill contingent turned out but virtually no one else at all, so Turbett had Her Imperial Majesty to himself. She, of course, had no knowledge of the machinations behind the scenes, nor could she know that it was a serious breach of precedent for the Ward to hunt on Ash Wednesday with both the hunt servants in scarlet. It was, in fact, just the sort of occasion she most enjoyed. There were no crowds, no staring populace, but a small select field composed only of her friends, all fired with the same enthusiasm for the chase and eagerness to ride as fast and as far as hounds and stag would let them.

Mr Turbett was lucky. It was a bitterly cold, raw day, but the outlier was found almost immediately and he provided them with a fast and flying forty minutes. When the stag was taken the Empress sent him a personal message of congratulation. Filled with triumph and delight Turbett, most unwisely, sent off a telegram to Morrogh telling him of the day's events and how much the Empress had enjoyed herself under his care and supervision.

The telegram was bad enough but when Morrogh opened his *Freeman's Journal* the following morning and read a full and fulsome account of the bye-day and the Empress's attendance and exploits he was very angry indeed. Immediately he sat down and wrote a letter to Turbett. This letter is far too long to be quoted in full. Mr Morrogh put his legal training to good use in its composition and it was a damning indictment of Turbett's conduct in the matter. The opening paragraph is sufficient to give an idea of the terms in which it was couched:

5, Great Denmark Street
Dublin, 28 February 1879

Dear Turbett,

The Bye-day for the Empress of Austria, Lord Spencer and their friends at Rathmolyon on Wednesday, which I see so fully reported in yesterday's *Freeman* has, in consequence of the exceptional privacy with which it was arranged, given much cause of offence to many of our best supporters, and in the interest of the Hunt, and to release the Committee of Management from blame in the matter, I think it needful to ask if you can give any explanation which will tend to remove or lessen this feeling of irritation existing in reference to it.

Turbett came back fighting but not, apparently, before he had consulted his own solicitor, for the letter gives every indication of having been drafted by a legal hand. Again the first paragraphs give the substance of the whole:

> 3 Bachelors Walk
> 20 March 1879
>
> Dear Sir,
> In reply to your letter of 28th ult., of 22 paragraphs, in which you have made nearly, if not altogether as many erroneous charges against me, I think it right to say with regard to:-
> (1) The day alluded to was not a 'Bye-day' but an ordinary day for the taking of an outlying deer in the usual way, and in such cases I have always had the management, and hitherto without being questioned, there was no exceptional privacy at all. It was your fault and not mine, as I shall hereafter point out.

The incident is only of importance in showing that, however much she wished to be a private person, and however hard she tried to bury herself from the public gaze and attention, because she was what she was and who she was she could never succeed. Because of her beauty, her graciousness, her presence and the name she bore, but more especially perhaps because of her thoughtlessness and unconscious tactlessness, jealousies, gossip, rivalries and spitefulness grew around her wherever she went. It would never have occurred to her, for instance, to enquire, or to have one of the suite enquire if it was entirely proper for Mr Turbett to bring out hounds on a bye-day apparently solely for her benefit, without reference to the Master and in his absence.

She herself, of course, knew nothing of the internecine war her presence had sparked off nor, perhaps, would she have cared very much if she had known since it did not affect her personally. Besides, she was just then engaged in falling in love with Ireland and the Irish, just as she had done with Hungary and the Hungarians. The people, gentry and peasant alike, were much the same in both countries. They were brave and feckless, humorous, dashing and dire, all the things she liked and admired most in men and women.

Her feelings were reciprocated. Everywhere the country people turned out to welcome and cheer her. Villagers, to show their respect for her, 'got into their seventh day clothes on the sixth day' whenever they heard she was about to pass through. There was an air, too, of holiday and expectancy wherever she went.

With all this spontaneous public reaction to a supposedly private visit, the occupants of the Viceregal Lodge were placed in a singularly difficult position. Already press criticism of their apparent cold-shouldering of their visitor was becoming stronger and more explicit. The lack of an official representative from the Castle to greet her on her arrival was especially pointed to as an apparent and deliberate slight. She herself made it quite clear that she had no desire to receive the Marlboroughs at Summerhill. Despite this the Castle now felt that something had to be done to give the visit at least some appearance of recognition. As a result it was arranged through Spencer, shortly before his departure, that the Duchess of Marlborough should attend the meet of the Meath Hounds at Holywood Rath. There presentations would take place and, it was hoped, cordial relations be established. Accordingly one special train from Dublin conveyed the Duchess, together with Lord and Lady Randolph Churchill, to Kilcock, while another brought the Empress to the same station from Summerhill.

The Duchess arrived early. She was met by Captain Thompson, the owner of Holywood Rath House, and made ready to meet her guest. She cannot, however, have had a very reassuring drive from Kilcock to the meet for again there were triumphal arches across the roads bearing such inscriptions as 'Come Back To Erin', and 'Welcome To The Empress'. The Duchess must have known too, that the throngs who lined the roads were not doing so in her honour and never had done even though she was the wife of the titular head of government and society in the country.

When the Empress arrived the presentations were duly made by Spencer. It would appear that, mindful of the criticisms and of the occasion, the Duchess did her best to mend matters. She was coldly informed that the Empress was incognito during her stay, that no official visit to Summerhill would be welcomed nor could the Countess of Hohenembs see her way to attending any of the Viceregal balls or receptions though she might consider sending one or more representatives. (She did, too: Heinrich Larisch and Captain Middleton!)

In any event the time to mend matters had then passed. Parnell had seized on the affair, seeing in it yet another opportunity to embarrass the administration. A day or two later he rose to speak in the House on the apparently innocuous vote of £206 for the Household of the Lord Lieutenant.

He thought—he said—that an item in the vote for the Chaplain's residence was something of a job and only a camouflage to allow the Chaplain to employ an assistant. If Ireland had its own Parliament he would be happy to support in proper state the Viceroy. All this preliminary was a camouflage of his own for the real sting he wanted to get in and which immediately followed: 'Only a few days ago', he thundered, 'when the Empress of Austria arrived in Ireland, there was no one present to receive Her Majesty from the Viceregal Lodge and this duty was left to be performed, as well as might be, by the Lord Mayor of Dublin.' After that broadside he moved a reduction in the vote.

The Chief Secretary, Mr James Lowther, rose immediately to protest that the reason no one waited on the Empress was that she came as a private person and that it would have been an intrusion to do so. Lowther was a brother of Lord Lonsdale, a noted thruster in the Shires who was to take the Woodland Pytchley the following year and who had known Elizabeth when she was at Cottesbrooke, so he would have had some knowledge of her ways. It is all but certain that it was on his advice the arrival was ignored. If so, that advice was faulty and his defence of it availed him nothing for the damage was done.

The following day *The Times* took the matter up. In a leader, no less, it issued the following smart reproof: 'The Chief Secretary's explanation of the omission to welcome the arrival of THE EMPRESS OF AUSTRIA was not to the purpose. Unofficial visits of foreign Sovereigns are welcomed though unofficially. Mr Parnell was entirely within his rights in taking the opportunity of the supplementary estimates to remind the Viceregal Household of courtly amenities . . .'

This moved Marlborough to instruct the Ulster King at Arms to make an immediate reply:

TO THE EDITOR OF THE TIMES

Sir,—Permit me to say a few words with reference to the remarks in your leading article to-day.

The Empress of Austria's sojourn in Ireland is in accordance with Her Majesty's express wish, of a strictly private character. Nevertheless, the Lord Lieutenant and the Duchess of Marlborough have been most solicitous to offer to Her Majesty every possible mark of consideration. The Viceregal carriages were, at Her Majesty's arrival, placed at her disposal, and their Graces were anxious to pay their personal respects to Her Majesty at Summerhill; but the Empress, adhering to her desire for privacy, declined the proffered attentions and, indeed, everything bearing the slightest semblance of a Royal or official reception.

Yours faithfully,

J. BERNARD BURKE, Ulster

Well might Marlborough echo the sentiments of one of his predecessors when thanking the Foreign Secretary for some words of encouragement: 'In England people altogether underrate the potency of the old hatred of the Saxon . . . The heart of this people is against us, and I see no prospect of improvement within any time that can be calculated . . . I am not given to despond but I need them [the words of encouragement] in the discharge of this most hateful and discouraging office.'

Well, too, might Spencer congratulate himself on having slipped away in time from a potentially most embarrassing situation, much of which, indeed, he had been responsible for creating, to return to the comparative peace of hunting in the Shires.

Meanwhile the originator of all the trouble was enjoying herself enormously. She hunted six days out of six and then, with only the visit to Maynooth with all its consequences intervening, nine days out of nine. Spencer had gone and the inner court was virtually reduced to three, Heinrich Larisch, Rudi Liechtenstein and Bay Middleton. Of these Middleton was unquestionably the most intimate. He was attentive, considerate and charming, the manic pranks abandoned, all the rough edges temporarily at any rate whittled away, at least in her presence. And, out hunting, it was he who showed her the way, gained for her the sport and excitement she craved, and made her days for her.

On the famous Turbett bye-day they had come to a flooded river. A field in front of the rest and alone with hounds—and Mr Turbett—Middleton had taken a pull to see if he should search for a better place than that which faced them. In answer she had smiled, shaken up The Widow and sailed over the water. Along with him she was one of the four out of a hundred to see the finish when the Meath Hounds killed their fox after a fast forty minutes from Bull Ring Gorse. To get there they had had to jump tired horses over a famous fence, the Ryndville Double, 'a great straight-cut embankment margined by wide dry ditches' which had been known to stop many a hopeful thruster. She had taken it without pausing and without the semblance of a mistake. A day or two later, with the Kildare, he had bored a hole for her at 'the famous Laragh fence, a big bank and ditch much over-grown with timber'. They had jumped it together and were never caught in 'a fast twenty minutes with the pack racing in a half circle to Courtown'.

He took some tremendous falls in doing all this. In mounting her on the best he had omitted to provide for himself as he should have done. He had twenty-five horses, after all, left behind in the Shires eating their heads off in a hunting box, North Lodge, which that season he was sharing with his fiancée's brother. The cost of providing another string of top-notchers for himself in Ireland would have been prohibitive even if he could have found them. Thus, in getting her to the front, he had to ask his horses questions they were frequently unable to answer and he was often on the floor.

'Captain Middleton', she wrote to the Emperor, 'had a very awkward beast, quite out of condition. The pace was very sharp and the obstacles high, so he was soon down. He came down again at a very high, steep bank.' And again: 'We came to a bank with a ditch and Captain Middleton fell in. While still standing on his head (*sic*) called out 'All right' quite cheerfully, and I got over perfectly easily. The ditch was very much overgrown, so his horse had made a mistake and jumped into the middle of it instead of over it, but mine could see the ditch through the hole which he made.'

Yet somehow, once again, despite the falls, he seemed to be always at her side when he was needed. Once more the name 'Bay' was seldom far from her lips and was spoken with particular affection. Now, if ever, one might have expected the union to be consummated. Yet it remains unlikely that they became lovers in the accepted physical sense.

In the first place the Victorians did not go in for al fresco physical frolics. The setting for their adulteries was the double bed. In any event Elizabeth was far too fastidious to indulge in untidy open-air coupling. If consummation occurred it must have taken place at Summerhill. At first sight it might appear that, with the inner court reduced to three old friends, the huge house, the loneliness and the privacy, there would have been every opportunity for illicit love.

Despite all these things, together with the gaiety, the intimacy, the fun, the long, languorous Irish nights, the physical relaxation of fit muscles after hunting, the closeness that comes from danger shared and surmounted, there were certain circumstances surrounding that house party which set it apart from others where bedroom doors opened often and all too easily. It has to be remembered that, however much she tried to avoid it, there was always in her presence the exclusiveness that stamped an empress and a Habsburg. In addition, Larisch and Liechtenstein were proud men from families heavy with quarterings, guardians, self-styled perhaps, but guardians nevertheless, of their Imperial mistress's name and reputation. They were, too, personal friends of the Emperor and, in the case of Liechtenstein at least, to some extent in his confidence. They would furiously have resented any forward move on Middleton's part unless its welcome by her was made so clear as to amount to a command. Her shy, withdrawn nature especially where matters physical were concerned must make it all but certain that this did not occur.

Besides, Middleton was a Victorian gentleman and as such lived by a code. It was a code that was rigidly interpreted and those who transgressed it were made outcasts instantly. One of its tenets, as has been said before, was that where the other party was of equal or higher standing physical union depended upon her open and evident availability. By no stretch of the imagination could Elizabeth be described as an available woman. She had already cut short friendships with those few who had tried to presume further with a freezing look and a cutting phrase. Middleton must have heard of these incidents which were common knowledge at court. He surely must also by then have realised, for he did not lack experience of women, that were he fortunate enough to be the man who did possess her, he might, by that very act of possession, end by losing her.

The Victorians, as Miss Anita Leslie says, regarded amour as a game. What they both were doing was playing this game—an exceptionally dangerous one in the circumstances—and playing it supremely well. The dangers, for him especially, were formidable indeed. The winning stakes were, quite simply, unobtainable. If he were in love with her, and there can be little doubt that he was, consummation of that love was, as has been said, so unlikely that it could be discounted. And continuation of their romantic association on its present basis, given the circumstances surrounding them, could hardly be expected to last more than another season or two at most. The losing hazards of prolonging it on its present terms were very great. Were he to overstep the mark sexually—and sexual strain and tension must have existed between them, handsome, healthy and ardent as they both were—he would have been ruined socially. In addition, though he was now without any doubt her favourite there was always with her the risk of losing favour from a cause that might well be all but imaginary. He must by now have known very well the fickle, mercurial moods of his goddess and how her love and affection could, from some transgression real or imagined, swing with startling suddenness to derision and aversion. Then, too, there was the question of his fiancée waiting in the wings now for over two years. Charlotte Baird was the daughter of one friend and the sister of another. She was said to be in a position to bring him £20,000 a year and his own means were not great for that day and age. Marie Larisch has said, and it may or may not be true, that the Empress told her Bay had virtually nothing to live on. Even if she did say this it must be remembered that 'nothing' to the Empress might well be a sufficiency to others for the resources then available to her were vast. For her 'small expenses' she received a yearly allowance of 200,000 gulden which was paid in monthly instalments and when she was away from home another 56,000 gulden a month was allotted to her. It was seldom in any one year that these sums sufficed and when they were exceeded Franz Joseph made up the deficiency without a murmur. The remark of a cynic at court that the pedestal of her suffering was a golden one was not therefore inapt. Middleton was certainly far from being one of the richest bachelors of the day but to one possessed of money on this scale any income he might have had would have seemed small indeed.

So they both skated with the greatest of delicacy over the thinnest of thin ice and avoided falling through. The Victorian upper classes, who loved games of every sort especially where social perils were involved, watched the process with delight and admiration.

This did not stop the gossip. However, since there was no Marie Larisch, no Rudolph, no ex-Queen of Naples at Summerhill it was not related back to the Empress. Indeed she gaily declared on a later occasion that the great advantage of Ireland was that there were no Royal Highnesses. With nothing, then, to interfere with her serenity and with Bay's help she rode herself into a reputation across Meath and Kildare fully as great as that she had gained in Northamptonshire. 'There is only *one* opinion about *her*', wrote the faithful Festetics, 'but, really, my hair is always standing on end.'

Countess Festetics was right on both counts. Elizabeth had caught and captivated the hearts of the Irish 'people, peer and peasants' with her beauty and prowess. But the list of the 'wounded' which made the Countess's hair stand on end was impressive enough. Mrs Morrogh broke her arm in a collision at a gateway; Bayzand, whose hands were never of the best and whose nerve was weakening with the years, could not at all acclimatise himself to jumping banks. He held on to his horse's head instead of freeing it at the take-off. This resulted in several falls, each more severe than the last, until finally he was carried away unconscious on an improvised stretcher. Lord Langford was scarcely ever out but he was down and spent most of the visit either limping or being strapped up from one injury or another.

Much of this grief resulted, of course, from the rivalry engendered by her presence. Lady Randolph Churchill came out with the Meath resolved to show her Imperial Majesty a thing or two. In endeavouring to cut out the work in a fast thirty minutes from Baltrasna she took two heavy falls and retired from the field. Nor did she accompany her husband the following day with the Kildare at Enfield where the Empress was given a truly regal welcome.

Despite all these accidents, during the eighteen days' hard hunting she put in the Empress herself only once suffered anything that resembled a fall. This was nearing the end of her stay when The Widow—renamed Summerhill in honour of Ireland, her enjoyment and her host—slipped on the top of a bank and almost came down on the far side. She jumped off and allowed the mare to recover. Middleton put her up again and they were back in the hunt with scarcely a minute lost.

Nor did she owe her success to the superiority of her mounts. To help out Middleton she shared Merry Andrew with him so she did not have the exclusive use of this splendid hunter. Domino, it is true, was a star but he and The Widow, good though they were, were not exceptional in a country of good performers. The Widow had, in fact, lost some of her speed and dash with age; she could be sticky enough at times and needed driving at her fences; while Cameo, probably the next best of the string, was the exact opposite, being almost too keen and a decidedly difficult conveyance in a trappy country. Yet they all came alike to her.

On one occasion, hacking home with Middleton after a day with the Ward, they passed Fairyhouse racecourse where the Irish Grand National—then run over banks—was held. She insisted on herself and Middleton jumping the course, which included the famous Ballyhack double. On returning home she gaily told the dinner party how much she had enjoyed it but that she did not think the fences as formidable as those she had encountered out hunting.

Middleton himself had a racing problem on his hands just then. One of the greatest ambitions of his life was to win the Grand National Hunt Steeplechase, the 'Amateurs Grand National', and that year he thought he might pull it off on Minotaur, Hugh Owen's mount in the Pytchley Hunt Cup the year before. The race was due to be run at Derby on 16 March. He knew very well that the lady might not take too kindly to his absenting himself from her side on a hunting day. Fortunately for him the weather had been wet and wintry throughout her stay and, since she insisted on braving it all day and every day, she paid the penalty by catching a heavy cold. Langyi insisted on her remaining in the house for a day or two and not hunting. Immediately Middleton took himself off to England and the racecourse. Exactly where the unfortunate Charlotte Baird came into his life at this time—if at all—must remain a matter of conjecture.

The Grand National Hunt Steeplechase was then run at a different meeting each year. Derby had been selected for this year's renewal. It was what was then called an 'enclosed' course as opposed to many others where the races were run over what amounted to a natural country with the fences cut and trimmed to help the pace a bit. This was held to improve the chances of the favourite, Bellringer, who had some form as a two-year-old on the flat. Middleton on Minotaur set off in front with the evident intention of cutting the others down. He fell at the fence beyond the stands, remounted and went into the lead again. But the fall put paid to his chances. At the last hurdle Bellringer, ridden by Arthur Coventry, had him collared. Bellringer went on to win and Golden Cross, ridden by another crack amateur, E. P. Wilson, also caught Minotaur on the run in; Middleton had to be content with third place out of sixteen runners.

The following day he pulled Minotaur out again in the Grand National Hunter's Plate. There were only two other runners and Minotaur was backed as a certainty, starting at 11–10 on. He was ten lengths ahead as they turned for home. Once more he could not quite pull it off. Skyscraper, ridden by Charlie Cunningham, another crack, who that year had the astonishing average of one win in every three rides, made up ground steadily and was with him at the last. Skyscraper ran up the fence and appeared to lose his chance but Cunningham, who was an exceptionally strong jockey, straightened him. With Minotaur faltering and the two men riding for all they were worth a terrific battle up the straight ensued. In the very last stride Cunningham got Skyscraper up to win by a head.

These races illustrate Middleton's failings as a jockey. He was too inclined to adopt forcing tactics for, just as in hunting, he liked to be in front, and he was not an effective finisher. Since he had tipped his mount widely in Ireland before he left and had almost certainly backed himself heavily to win, the Empress's indisposition was an unfortunate one for him.

She, however, had refused to stay indoors for more than a day, especially as it would have meant missing a St Patrick's Day Hunt. On the Saint's Day and in the absence of Middleton Mr Morrogh, 'his face beaming with satisfaction', had the pleasure and privilege of piloting her with the Ward. He provided her with an outstanding hunt.

The meet was at Culmullen Cross Roads. There were triumphal arches and welcoming banners everywhere. The Empress took even more particular care of her toilette than usual and turned herself out in the acme of style as fitting to the occasion. She wore 'a gold-buttoned *matclasse* habit, the buttons bearing the Imperial arms, open in front showing a white necktie adorned with a pin, and a very narrow brimmed riding hat. In the breast of her habit was a sprig of shamrock.'

Right well, too, did she carry the national emblem for after forty-five minutes of the best only she, Morrogh and four others were in at the finish. At the end of it Mr Humphries, with whose Cavan Staghounds she had stolen away to have a quiet day shortly before her indisposition and whose big bloodlike bay hunter she had much admired, came up, swept off his hat and presented the horse to her as a gift and a tribute to the way she had gone.

Morrogh was so delighted that he promptly laid on two more bye-days for her in quick succession, but he lost his position as pilot for by this time Middleton was back.

She really loved the gallop with the Ward for with them there was no hanging about or waiting as in fox-hunting. Only a minute or so after the enlargement of the stag the field could sit down and ride for their lives. So her days were filled with pure happiness. There was no time now for boredom, melancholy or introspection. All was go and gaiety, tribute and laughter both in the field and at Summerhill. Under this treatment her beauty took on a fresh bloom. Her amber eyes glowed and her complexion was as fresh and clear as a girl's. A visiting diplomat seeing her enter Summerhill after a day's hunting wrote that he refused to accept the truth of her age. She looked at most, he said, a young and radiant thirty-two.

Then once more the world and its cares came crowding in. On 20 March the Summerhill telegram bore the news of the terrible disaster at Szegedin, the flooding and the many deaths. The plight of the poor and the defenceless, suffering and loss of life always called out the best in her. Her place was there at her husband's side and for once she knew it. She announced immediately that she would cut short her visit and return to Austria as soon as arrangements could be made. 'I feel it would be better for me to leave now, and you will be better pleased, too,' she wrote to the Emperor. 'It is the greatest sacrifice I can make, but in such conditions it is necessary.'

On the following morning she went out with the Meath at Dunshauglin for her last day's hunting in Ireland. The news of her departure had got abroad and once more there were crowds, banners and arches with the motif 'Come back to Erin' predominating. She was, in fact, determined to do just that and had given instructions that the private chapel in Summerhill was not to be dismantled and that her horses were to remain there under the care of MacDonald.

The day at Dunshauglin was a bad one—she had little luck with the Meath that year—and she cut it short, returning to Summerhill a few minutes after midday. Before she had left for hunting that morning she had given instructions for an enormous buffet to be prepared and now she issued invitations for everyone who sat in a saddle that day, no matter who he was, peer or pauper, farmer, second horseman, rough-rider or Castle ADC, to take luncheon with her at Summerhill. Most of the field availed themselves of her hospitality which continued throughout the afternoon. This was the sort of open-handed gesture to all alike which endeared her so much to the plain people of Ireland and made them contrast her behaviour with Viceregal exclusiveness.

Next morning she left for Dublin by special train. A huge crowd turned up at Broadstone station to wish her Godspeed and the police were unable to prevent an invasion of the station although they had locked the gates and attempted to block the approaches. They had some difficulty, too, in escorting her through the cheering throng to the waiting carriages. Then she was driven to the Shelbourne Hotel. Here the Viceroy had his first and only meeting with her. Mindful of the trouble caused by his ignoring of her arrival Marlborough had determined not to allow her departure to cause him similar embarrassment, to say nothing of further questions in the House. Colonel Forster, the Master of the Horse who had hunted much with Her Majesty and gained some favour with her, was put in charge of the presentation and he managed it with his usual tact. The Marlboroughs drove to the Shelbourne shortly before six o'clock and were granted a brief and formal audience.

Then came that touch of the extraordinary which was never far away from whatever she did. She had arranged to have a farewell dinner with Middleton in the Shelbourne before she left for the special steamer which had been chartered for her voyage across the channel. Here, presumably, farewells were to be said and future meetings arranged. It is at all events exceedingly significant that Middleton was so honoured and that neither her host, Lord Langford, nor the head of her household were included in the invitation. But empresses, even those as unconventional as Elizabeth, did not dine *à deux* in hotels on public or indeed any other occasions. Elizabeth's choice of a chaperone fell upon Forster, probably because during his stay she had learnt to admire his discretion and appreciate his charm.

The Duchess of Marlborough came in some manner to hear of the invitation to her Master of Horse and she profoundly disapproved of it. She informed Forster that on the evening in question he would be expected to dine at a formal function at the Castle. This, of course, was to all intents and purposes a command and ranked as one as both the Duchess and Forster well knew. Forster, however, was not an experienced courtier for nothing. He compared the times of the respective invitations and saw that with a little hurrying here and there he could fulfil both. So he solved his dilemma by attending and eating both meals—dinner at the Castle and supper with the Empress.

Although the Marlboroughs had done their duty towards her and been dismissed, which was one formal function disposed of, Elizabeth still had to deal with the question of how she should pay the respects which were clearly due to the English royal family on her way across England. Needless to say she wanted to avoid this task if she could. Queen Victoria, whom by now she cordially disliked, was, she learnt to her great satisfaction, safely abroad and out of the way, but the Prince of Wales was in London and would expect to present himself to her. Even this meeting, however, she expected to prove both boring and tedious and she looked for a way of putting it off. In attempting to find one she adopted the totally disingenuous stratagem of appealing to the Emperor's sense of economy. 'The Queen will not be back from Italy when I leave,' she wrote. 'Do you really want me to stop in London? I would gladly avoid it to save hotel bills. Then I should have made the whole journey here and back without going to an hotel.'

In the end she found a compromise which was, as usual, blazingly indiscreet and pleased nobody. On her way by train through London she paused for fifteen minutes at Addison Road Station, Kensington. During that hurried quarter of an hour the Prince of Wales called upon her. Short and unsatisfactory to both parties, this interview cannot have done anything to further protocol or cement relations between the two royal families, for the Empress appears to have given every indication that she regarded it as an intrusion and only wanted to be on her way. After the Prince left the special train continued to Dover where yet another specially chartered steamer was waiting. There were no further interviews or interruptions until she reached Vienna. The expenses of those few weeks in Ireland reached the staggering total of 158,337 gulden and 48 kreuzer. The saving of a day's hotel bill in Claridge's would scarcely have made much difference to that huge sum. Once more the Emperor paid up without a murmur. He was glad only to have his beautiful Sisi safely at his side once more looking lovelier than ever and undamaged in limb or feature by the perils of the hunting field.

The bloom of radiant physical health and the glow of remembered happiness was still upon her when they celebrated their silver wedding that summer. As always she hated the ceremonies. Public feeling against her long absences and her preoccupation with things other than matters of state, especially horses, was just beginning to come out into the open. One writer commented that at a jubilee it was usual to celebrate twenty-five years of *ménage* but this one was after twenty-five years of *manège*.

The remark was as apt as it was witty but for once, still wrapped in euphoria, she only laughed when she was told of it.

CHAPTER EIGHT

Come back to Erin

That summer she plunged with greater enthusiasm than ever into equestrian matters. Ireland was a hunting paradise to which she was determined to return. To fit herself for the coming visit she threw herself into the task of making herself an even better horsewoman than before. She studied *haute école* and mastered the *piaffe*, the *passage*, and the *capriole*. That done she brought to Gödollo an expert called Baucher who had invented new movements and had him instruct her in them until her performance was faultless. During this instruction she kept a book of notes on her progress. 'Changing legs while threading my way in and out of the benches at a gallop' she noted to be exceedingly difficult, and she was in advance of her time when she set down that one must 'throw your body forward at the take-off when jumping'. In addition to the personal instruction she had given her by Baucher she bought and had sent to her books on horses and horsemanship from all over the world. In these she studied current theories of riding and compared ideas gleaned from different countries. The English *Racing Calendar* was also subscribed to and sent to her, presumably so that she could follow Bay Middleton's career on the racecourse.

After her departure from Ireland Middleton had returned to North Lodge to finish the season and had resumed, too, his rivalry with Doggie Smith. 'Captain Smith is in his usual form; Captain Middleton in his accustomed place,' Brooksby, the famous hunting correspondent, once wryly remarked as he watched them riding out a hunt. He was also determined to get a race out of Minotaur. This he did at Leicester where he won the Hunters' Steeplechase. He then promoted Minotaur to handicap company and ran him at Brocklesby in the Open Steeplechase. At the open ditch Minotaur came down and broke his neck, giving Middleton, too, a bad fall that put him out of action for some weeks. There is no doubt he was very hard on his horses about that time. To replace Minotaur and while he was out of the saddle he bought a young horse by Kingsley, dam by Windischgraetz, out of Light of the Harem, which he called Lord of the Harem. All Bay's horses were splendidly named and Lord of the Harem was to prove later on the most successful of all his racehorses; on him he ran up a long series of victories, no fewer than sixteen wins out of as many starts in the years 1882–1884.

So far as can be ascertained he was not at Gödollo that autumn, but, according to Marie Larisch, the 'muscle water' continued to be despatched 'in gallons' to him and they continued to correspond. Elizabeth had not left her horses behind in Ireland for nothing and she was longing to get back. She was now forty-one and the intimations of mortality, particularly in the shape of the rapidly emerging Rudolph who was twenty-one, were becoming stronger every year, indeed almost every month. Middleton, nine years younger than she, with his unquestioning adoration, renewed her youth, which Rudolph emphatically did not.

Rudolph himself, probably because there were fewer Corinthians about that season than usual, was much at Gödollo. The shooting was excellent, the bags were enormous and he was happy because he was killing things. The combination of Habsburg and Wittelsbach blood had produced in him a real and abiding lust for destruction, especially of living things, quite different from the impersonal killing for sport which characterised the English country gentleman of the period. Rudolph's lust to kill would have been despised by Middleton and his caste as unskilful, bounderish and foreign, and his mother, who loved wild things and animals generally, deplored and feared it. This trait coupled with a death wish and helped and exaggerated by the venereal infections incurred through his other excesses was, of course, to have tragic consequences for himself and the dynasty.

That autumn, apart from conducting enormous *battues* at Gödollo—it was during just such a one of these that he shot and killed the beater—he was searching for a role and trying to find himself. Although he was now of full age his father would not allow him access to state papers or the slightest say in matters of government. He was no fool; he saw that dynastic attitudes were becoming so embalmed that they must ultimately destroy themselves. He was also sensible enough to realise that the present faint stirrings of liberal ideas within the Empire towards which his father was turning a face of stone were bound to spread and permeate the whole structure of society, and that some accommodation with them would have to be made. With all that in mind he prepared a long paper on the subject for the Emperor. It is significant, however, that it was never submitted. He was still very much in awe of his father and dreaded the repercussions that might follow its reception. Nor did he ask his mother to intervene for by now he and she had virtually ceased to communicate. Even had he done so it is unlikely that she would have helped. She was, just then, out of sympathy both with him and her surroundings. The sport at Gödollo quite failed to approach that which she had enjoyed galloping across Northamptonshire or the green fields of Meath. Sickened by the wholesale slaughtering of game indulged in by Rudolph and his friends and by the sexual intrigues in which he was involved, she was daily gripped by the longing to return to the freshness and simplicity of Ireland where she could revel in the open admiration and simple companionship of hard-riding men like Middleton and Morrogh.

The efforts of Baroness Vetsera, sister of the Baltazzis, aided and abetted by the mischievious Marie Larisch, to ingratiate herself with Rudolph were the talk of the court. The ceremonial duties which Elizabeth had to perform in Vienna became ever more stultifying. The days were flying by. However hard she might try to hide the fact from herself her looks and her figure would not last forever. Nor would the days when she could ride in front with the best on the best. Boredom and dissatisfaction possessed her.

My dearest Ida,
She wrote to the Countess Ferenczy from Munich:

Thanks be to God here is a day over; I find it painful and trying to be here all alone, with no one to talk to. I cannot tell you how much I miss you . . . write and tell me as much as possible, rather today than tomorrow. I would like to journey to the land of dreams but that will never happen.

Escape—that, as always, was the thing. Since there was no land of dreams Ireland was the best substitute. Already Bay Middleton had received instructions to buy more horses. He had crossed over to consult with MacDonald and Tom Healy, the rough-rider and with dealers whom he knew. Several purchases had been made, one of which was a magnificent blood-like bay whom she had given instructions was to be named 'The Bay'. To accommodate these an additional stable-block at the expense of the Imperial purse had been built on to the Summerhill yard. 'Come back to Erin' was going to be rather more than a dream. Yet, even now, it is hard to see just how she managed it.

Ireland was by then in a ferment. Already agrarian unrest was threatening hunting and several packs were considering stopping altogether. The Meath with which, along with the Ward, she intended mostly to hunt, had as its neighbour the Westmeath whose confines stretched to the Shannon borders right in the heart of the disaffected area. The future of the sport in Westmeath was in jeopardy and no one could tell when these pressures would extend further eastward.

It was true that Parnell, with his unique ability to touch the raw spots of the establishment and to create trouble out of the most innocent-seeming situations, was in America. But this visit to America had been made with the avowed intention of collecting funds and everyone knew what those funds, once amassed, were to be used for. The Marlboroughs were, naturally enough, both perturbed and annoyed at her proposal to return. Much worse, Queen Victoria was greatly displeased. That was a time, long forgotten today, when other nations wished to stand well with England. The echoes of Palmerstonian diplomacy were still strong. It was inconceivable to Queen, court and cabinet that Franz Joseph should permit the repetition of a visit which was known to have caused annoyance and had a potential of very considerable political disturbance. When 'Pretender' Parnell, as the Queen scornfully dubbed him, would return he was certain to find ways of making capital out of the Empress's presence in Ireland. At best it gave the Irish an opportunity to point a finger of scorn at the English reigning house. This dared not allow one of its members to set foot in the country at that time, yet a foreign royalty could move amongst them without escort or protection, sure of her safety and assured of a rapturous welcome.

Franz Joseph was an insensitive man, but he was a monarch and must in some degree at least have appreciated the feelings of fellow rulers. Why he sanctioned this second visit remains a mystery to this day. Probably, as with most decisions, it was made through a mixture of motives. First he could never—or very rarely—refuse his Sisi anything; secondly, she had long ago made clear that the terms on which she renounced a right to interfere in matters of state were that he should not meddle with her pleasures of riding and travelling; thirdly, communications in those days were slow and cumbersome and rulers depended almost entirely on information from their ambassadors, sent by these communications, as to conditions in other countries. For reasons both of prestige and defence the English were never anxious to advertise abroad their difficulties with Ireland, and that, in effect, their writ no longer ran in that country. Nor had either cabinet or crown ever made explicit their disapproval of the visit or its predecessor. There had been mutterings and mumblings but these had mostly been confined to inner circles of court and diplomacy. It is of course true that had Karolyi been astute enough he should have learnt of these and reported them. But Karolyi was a Hungarian aristocrat of great wealth and independence and a sportsman. All his inclinations would have been to please the Empress and gratify her wishes. It is probable that in his despatches he either omitted altogether or else watered down the strength of the feelings at the Court of St James's against the visit. Finally, Franz Joseph was just then grappling with the consequences of the Russo-Turkish war, the treaty of San Stefano and the German-Austrian alliance, which was Andrassy's last great gesture in diplomacy before his fall. Events in Ireland, indeed in the British Isles, must have seemed very far away and certainly of secondary importance to immediate central European concerns.

At all events, as usual, she got her way. As the Countess of Hohenembs once more she left Vienna by special train, though this time the incognito was thinner than ever since there was a semi-official send-off with Franz Joseph and Rudolph on the station to bid her Godspeed. There was no welcome for her at Dover, however, and no interruption for state calls or visits to the journey of the second special which whisked her across England at all possible speed. By five minutes to ten on the morning following her arrival at Dover, the steamer *Shamrock* with her on board berthed at North Wall, Dublin.

Her immediate suite was even smaller than the previous year for Heinrich Larisch was ill and could not travel. It consisted of Rudi Liechtenstein, Countess Festetics, Nopsca, Langyi, the doctor, and Linger, the secretary. Spencer, this time, did not accompany her. There was a whiff of political change in the air and with it the possibility of preferment for him. He wisely stayed away.

The Marlboroughs, this year, were not going to allow any criticism on the score of ignoring her to appear in the public prints. They sent along Colonel Forster, with Colonel Crofton and Captain Campbell, two of the ADCs, to greet her. The Lord Mayor was there, too, although she had refused his offer of full civic recognition, together with representatives of the railway company. Otherwise the platform was almost empty save for her host, Lord Langford, and, at her special request, Bay Middleton. It was Middleton who was at her side as they crossed the platform and it was he who entered the royal carriage immediately behind her. Then came Rudi Liechtenstein, Langford, and the rest of the small suite. She could scarcely be said to be travelling light for in a goods special which followed her own train were almost forty tons of her personal luggage. In that luggage was an elaborate gift for the hierarchy at Maynooth which, when it was presented, was to score another black mark against her in England.

At Kilcock she was given another royal welcome, albeit this time somewhat muted for an edict had gone forth from the Castle that triumphal arches and suchlike could cause a breach of the peace and the Royal Irish Constabulary had seen to their suppression. There were, however, huge Austrian and Bavarian flags at the station and nothing could stop the people turning out to cheer the gracious and lovely lady who had won their hearts the year before.

As was her custom, she asked to be driven immediately to the stables and there she inspected the stud. The first horse she required to be pulled out for her inspection was The Bay which for some reason was stabled apart from the others. She expressed herself delighted with him and laughed about his name with his namesake. Then, Bayzand at her side with a dish of sliced carrots, she went through the whole lot, Middleton's and Liechtenstein's horses as well as her own. When that was done and suitable compliments paid to grooms and attendants as to their charges she, Middleton and Langford walked to the house and went in to luncheon.

On this visit all pretence about 'The Countess of Hohenembs', although this remained as her official incognito, was abandoned. She was openly and everywhere in print and amongst personalities referred to and deferred to as 'The Empress'. And this time, though the immediate suite was small, the retinue which accompanied her was enormous. That first luncheon, apart from those mentioned who took the meal with her, twenty-five persons sat down in the steward's room and sixty-five in the servants' hall, making a total entourage of ninety men and women to serve her wishes and wait upon her pleasure.

In contrast to the previous year when there had been snow on the ground, in 1880 she arrived in brilliant sunshine. It was warm and mild as only Ireland can sometimes be in early February. Summerhill was set on a small eminence in a noticeably flat country. From its windows on that beautifully clear day with the sun striking colours from the countryside she could look out over blue vastnesses stretching to the sea on one side and away to the borders of the Shannon and the troubled lands that lay beyond on the other.

Immediately luncheon was over she announced her intention of riding out. Bayzand was instructed to have Domino saddled and she went upstairs to change from her travelling clothes into a habit. She had been on the move now by train and boat for over thirty-six hours' uninterrupted travelling, yet she wanted no rest. The spur and stimulation of friendship and adoration and the call of action always drove her on. Once she was caught up in its unleashing the nervous energy of the highly-strung would not allow her to pause or relax. When this happened she did not remotely resemble the woman known to the Viennese court as a moody, withdrawn creature given to weaknesses, vapours and half-imagined illnesses. Had they seen her then they would scarcely have recognised her. Nor, perhaps, would her husband. But he would have loved her all the more and might, just possibly, have come some way towards understanding her. Their tragedy was that he could never forget he was a Habsburg and she could never learn to be one.

As it was she walked down to the stables unaccompanied. Bayzand was waiting for her with Domino saddled and ready. In the stableyard she was joined by the man who had made and was making all this happiness possible for her—Bay Middleton.

She wore a dark blue habit and a Tyrolean hat with a little feather in it. To his and indeed to any eyes she must have looked enchanting. Not content with jumping Domino over a few fences to make certain that she had not forgotten the grip and swing of jumping an Irish bank she returned to the stables and had four of her other horses pulled out in succession and schooled each of them. Langford came along after a little while and joined in the fun. He and Middleton must have been glad enough to give their horses a chance of looking at banks for both had been hunting in the Shires up till then and had only a few horses between them who had seen banks at all. Middleton, especially, either because there had not been time, or because his purse was running short, or simply since he had bought the best in the country for her and omitted to provide for himself, was desperately short of horses that had any experience at all of Irish hunting. Both he and Langford were to pay for this failure adequately to mount themselves, Langford the more dearly, in bruises, breakages and loss.

All the same the omens seemed set fair for another enormously successful visit. The weather was wonderful; the company was composed of tried and trusted friends; the Empress did not look a day older; Middleton had lost none of his panache, gallantry and unconcealed admiration for her; her horses were fit and ready to carry her across any country in the three kingdoms. She announced that she would open her account with her beloved Ward, tomorrow, at Batterstown, riding Domino.

And, almost immediately, things began to go wrong.

Leonard Morrogh and his followers greeted her with delight. All was well at first. The stag ran straight and fast. Middleton, as usual, had himself and the Empress bang in the right place and, along with Morrogh and Brindley, they were in the select few in the very front.

Behind them, however, other things were happening. Chicken Hartopp had a fall and broke his collarbone and Bayzand, no better over banks this year than the season before, came down with his horse on top of him. His ankle was crushed and he was in considerable pain. So, for the second time within twelve months, he was borne off the field of the Ward on a gate. In addition, as she reported to the Emperor: 'Rudi Liechtenstein came down too, but did not hurt himself, and our host, Lord Langford, fell on his face and has not been able to swallow very well since.'

Much worse than that, however, was to come. Towards the end of the hunt someone, nobody ever discovered just who it was or how it happened, cannoned into Domino when jumping a fence. As he landed he went dead lame and the Empress jumped off.

Middleton came back to her and got down himself. He found the horse almost unable to walk and thought the injury was in his shoulder. With some difficulty they brought him to a neighbouring farmhouse and then looked round for help. Fortunately the second horses came up just then and they mounted these.

Almost an hour later the reporter from *Freeman's Journal* who was waiting in the yard at Summerhill to send in his account of the day's doings was horrified to see the Empress and Middleton come clattering in, both of them looking harassed and worried. Middleton was leading a riderless horse.

MacDonald was instructed to telegraph for a vet on the special Imperial line. Middleton ordered out two fresh horses and grooms were summoned to come and help with the injured Domino. There was, however, no transport for the grooms, so Middleton immediately proposed commandeering the reporter's outside car. Thereupon the driver was summoned to the Empress's side. 'Yer Majesty, I'm engaged to them gentlemen there,' he said, indicating with his whip the reporter and his assistant.

She walked over to where the men were standing and in her presence the driver asked what he should do. 'Anything and everything Her Majesty requires,' the reporter said gallantly. As he said it his newsman's eye noticed how distressed she looked though all the time thoughts of lost deadlines and editorial censure were whirling through his head as he saw the grooms mounting his car.

Middleton, MacDonald and the outside car all went off into the night leaving the Empress alone in the yard with the two men. 'Her Majesty looked like a spectre in the dull twilight, her slim tall figure standing out in bold relief against the windows of the lighted stables.' She crossed over to them, bowed, and thanked them most graciously for their help. She would do all she could, she said, to see that they suffered no further inconvenience or other consequence for so readily coming to her assistance. After that she turned and walked unaccompanied to the house. Her very presence, the reporter recalled, left a sort of warm glow behind her, and he felt, as men did when she thanked them, that come what might, he had been well rewarded for what he had done.

She was desperately worried about the injury to her favourite and the news about him was no better that night. Bayzand, his ankle packed with ice, was lying 'groaning in bed' and altogether that evening was a gloomy one in Summerhill.

The next day with the Meath, Tom Healy being promoted personal attendant in place of Bayzand, was uneventful, but the day after, with the Ward, Lord Langford killed one of his English horses. It went into a farside ditch when trying to clear a bank without changing on it. Middleton on one of his very nearly did the same. He landed in a similar ditch with his horse on top of him. She came back to help with the result that they both lost the hunt. 'He was soon out of the ditch himself', she wrote, 'though somewhat out of breath or, as they say here, with the wind knocked out of him, and by the time he had pulled his horse out again of course the hounds were far away.' The very next day Middleton took such a fall into a lane that he knocked himself clean out, which took some doing. She caught his horse, came back and again lost the hunt.

He began to be down so often that when he fell he would

shout to her to go on with Tom Healy. This she did and in a day or so, such was her confidence in herself, her nerve and her horses, that she was soon taking her own line. She had falls, too, but nothing shook her courage or impaired her skill. 'Middleton and I fell . . . but the ground was quite soft. Several people must have fallen in so Tom told me later but I did not see them for of course I rode on at once. I saw Lord Langford standing by another ditch fishing for his horse.' Langford is said to have been in a bad temper throughout the visit. Judging by his experiences out hunting he seems to have had reason for it.

With Middleton being let down by his horses and the Empress going almost as well when not under his wing her fame grew even greater than before. And, of course, everyone, from the highest to the lowest did what they could to assist her. She never carried money but Mr Morrogh noticed that she always came out with a stock of the finest Viennese lace handkerchiefs somehow secreted in her form-fitting habits. If anyone performed a service for her such as pulling down an obstruction in a gap or opening a gate she would drop one of these handkerchiefs nearby as a reward and keepsake.

Middleton's misfortunes continued. 'It was not a very nice jump', she wrote of one occasion to the Emperor, 'so I waited to see how Middleton would take it. But instead of jumping straight his mare pitched head over heels to the left into the water where the ditch with a lot of tangled bushes formed the corner of the road. Since the way was free before me, (he was still making the holes for her despite the inadequacy of his mounts and it took some nerve to do this when hounds were running) I got over safely as did Tom.'

That was the night some wag composed the oft-repeated jingle, and at dinner they stood and sang it to her as she entered the long dining-room at Summerhill:

> The Queen of the Chase!
> The Queen! Yes, The Empress!
> Look, look, how she flies,
> With a hand that never fails
> And a pluck that never dies.
> The best man in England can't lead her—he's down!
> 'Bay' Middleton's back is done beautifully brown.

Hark horn and hark holloa!
Come on for a place!
He must ride who would follow
The Queen of the Chase!

The best man in England Middleton might have been but he was not, just then, the best man in Ireland and he knew it. Others now were in the forefront of those good hunts with the Ward where he should have been. He could always take a joke against himself. He laughed at the song and indeed repeated the part about his coat being brown.

But, being the man he was, he did not much care for taking second place in any sporting pursuit, especially hunting. Matters came to a head when a brown horse he had brought over from England simply refused to jump the country at all. Even he, with all his strength and skill, aided by some uninhibited language, could not make this horse take on an Irish bank or attempt to do so. Having shouted to the Empress to go on with Tom he found himself in the humiliating position of accompanying the road-riders, the funkers and those who hunted for show. With Tom in charge Elizabeth saw out the hunt and Middleton's leg was pulled again and unmercifully in the Victorian way that night at dinner.

It has been mentioned that the losing hazards of Middleton's association with the Empress were immense. If this sort of thing went on for any length of time he might encounter yet another of them. In her unpredictable way it was only too possible for her to decide that since he would not or could not mount himself well enough to pilot her she would find someone else. As it happens she did not and the matter never arose, which alone shows the strength of the feeling she had for him. She was full of solicitude and sympathy. But, like everyone else, he could never be sure of her. Moreover, although there were risks in continuing the association, there were great advantages, too. There was much of the shrewd Scot in Middleton. Always he had at least half an eye on the main chance and where opportunities lay for financial and social gain. The prestige accruing to his name as the man selected to pilot the Empress and maintained in that position through four seasons, was immense. It could not have been other than tremendously gratifying to him to know that some of the fierce light which surrounds a crowned head was reflected upon him. In fact, it is, of course, the association of his name with hers which has earned him his niche, however small, in history. His name now appears in virtually every volume on the latter years of the Habsburg Empire. Had he not been her pilot he would have been remembered, if at all, for a generation or so amongst hunting people and in hunting lore as an eccentric character and a brilliant horseman. Who now, outside the faded pages of hunting diaries or reports, recalls Doggie Smith or Chicken Hartopp?

Apart altogether from his place in the social forefront there were financial advantages, too, and he was not the man to overlook them. It was known everywhere that he bought her horses for her, and that she sometimes hunted his. This vastly increased the prices he could ask when selling, for buyers were only too anxious to say: 'One of Bay's, y'know. I believe the Empress hunted him.' And, if he was purchasing, the fact that he was buying for her would not, to say the least, detract from his chances of getting something for himself at the right price.

For all these reasons the business of being left in the rear and becoming, for once, something of a butt to the wits at Summerhill (and it has to be remembered, too, that there were still about those envious ones all too ready to spread it abroad that he was losing his nerve) could not be allowed to continue. He took immediate steps to remedy the situation and went into consultation with MacDonald. They both disappeared for a couple of days. When they returned they brought back with them a big, bloodlike grey which took up its quarters with Bay's string. No one quite knew whether it had been bought, borrowed or hired, but it was just the sort of horse he liked to ride and it restored him to his rightful position at the head of affairs.

Immediately everything took a turn for the better. Domino's injury was found to be nothing like so serious as had first been thought, and he was soon back in work. Even if The Bay was not proving a great success and Summerhill, originally The Widow, had been temporarily discarded on the grounds of age and slowness at her fences, the other horses, Cameo, Ashtown and the rest, were all going splendidly.

Once more she was writing gaily and with animation to the Emperor about her adventures: 'A lady called Miss Hussey fell in front of me and she and her grey simply rolled over and over.' 'Though we were really invited to hunt the fox with the Kildare, the gentlemen decided yesterday that we must go stag-hunting instead, if only to give the slip to all the inquisitive persons who come out in crowds by special train whenever I am expected anywhere at a meet. All the evening and early this morning Middleton and Lord Langford were laughing at the thought of taking them in like this.' Indeed this was just the sort of escapade she loved—to slip away and cheat the staring crowds. And she found more sympathy for this behaviour amongst the inconsequential Irish than anywhere else. The crowds did not mind; in a way they loved her all the more for her unpredictability, and the real hunting people approved. 'All the rag, tag and bobtail' had turned up to stare at the Empress, one hunting diarist recorded of this day, and added with satisfaction: 'They were disappointed.'

That day, Middleton, she recorded, was down again: 'He remained with his foot caught in the stirrup, in a way that was almost more alarming than the other day, for his horse wanted to go on, but my Tom saved him again.'

Middleton, had he seen it, would hardly have been flattered by the description of his being saved by the groom but Healy, profiting by Bayzand's continued absence on the injured list, was rapidly winning his way into the Empress's affections. She was delighted with him, the way he rode and the manner in which he had looked after her when Middleton's horses were letting him down. Soon he was taken permanently into Imperial service and his position confirmed as Bayzand's successor, at least in the hunting field. So, with a new worshipper at the shrine in 'My Tom', the days went on, all gaiety, good fun and success. Middleton's falls became fewer and they both rode themselves into even greater fame and glory than before.

The first Sunday of the visit saw her attending Mass at Maynooth once again. This time Middleton did not accompany her for the arrangements were much more formal. It was almost a semi-official visit and she came bearing gifts. Linger was sent on to announce her arrival and she was accompanied in her carriage by Countess Festetics. A second carriage followed bringing Nopsca and Rudi Liechtenstein.

Nopsca made the presentation formally to the Vice-

President of the college, the Very Reverend Dr Walsh. It was a munificent article indeed but, as usual with her, she had allowed the occasion to go slightly awry, and the symbolism of the gift was off-key. Possibly she had given the wrong instructions when authorising its manufacture or listened to incorrect advice or, what was even more likely, given the vaguest of instructions and taken no advice at all. In any event what she presented to the College of the Irish priesthood at Maynooth was: 'A silver equestrian statue of St George slaying the dragon, some three feet high and weighing four hundred and sixty ounces, mounted on an ebony pedestal embossed with the imperial arms. St George, mounted, is shown in the act of slaying the dragon with his sword.'

Since St George was the patron saint of England and to many minds at the time the dragon could well have represented Ireland and the Irish, the gift could scarcely have been more inappropriate. St Patrick (Ireland) casting out the snakes (England) would have been far more acceptable to Irish eyes. However, the warmest thanks were made to her by the Vice-President in taking the gift and it remains in Maynooth to this day as an elegant if tactless footnote to history.

It may have been hinted to her that the symbolism was not quite what the nationalistic clergy of Maynooth would have expected, for the following week she made arrangements for a further presentation to be prepared. A most elaborate set of vestments was ordered in Dublin. This comprised 'chasuble, stole, maniple, veil, burse, of cloth of gold with orphreys of green silk embroidery, and edging of green silk with small gold shamrocks . . . At the base three shields are embossed bearing the arms of Austria, Bavaria and Hungary. They are surmounted with the Austrian crown. The name "Elizabet" with the date "1880" is worked on to the lining near the lower edge of the back.'

If there were some at Maynooth who deprecated the tactless nature of the gift, the semi-official status of the visit, the attendant publicity coupled with the extraordinary presentation of an image of an English saint to an Irish college not noted for furthering friendliness to the Crown, gave far greater offence in England. Other threats to her peace of mind and happiness were gathering force, too.

In America Parnell had made full use of the privilege granted to him of addressing the House of Representatives. He availed himself of the opportunity to make an unbridled attack upon English policy in Ireland couched in the terms of vituperation he knew so well how to command and he coupled this with a scurrilous onslaught on the Marlboroughs in both their private and official capacities. Now he was about to cross the Atlantic on his return to Ireland, his pockets full of American gold, determined to intensify his campaign of harassment and agrarian unrest and with the means to do it. The time was not an auspicious one for a foreign sovereign to be enjoying the plaudits of the very populace and priesthood who were then engaged in execrating the English. By a paradox which they recognised and disliked it was not the authorities who were embarrassed at having to provide protection for her but rather they required protection from the fact of her presence and what was implicit in it.

Blissfully unconscious of all this, Elizabeth announced that she had never enjoyed herself so much nor loved any country better than Ireland. She had already told her host that one of its attractions were that there were no royal highnesses. Everyone was natural; everyone loved her. Her horses were going tremendously well and Bay Middleton was back in his best form. She was determined, she said, to return every year for the hunting. With that in view she had four of her horses sent to Ireland from Austria. When they arrived they were handed over to Tom Healy to be taught to jump banks and to be made ready for next season. Middleton, too, was asked to look out for experienced hunters to strengthen her string so that there should be no shortage of horses when she returned. He and MacDonald kept their eyes open and let it be known that they were in the market. Very soon he had bought for her two well-known performers, Hard Times from Captain Steeds, the polo player, and The Doctor from Lord Howth, both at long prices. It was, however, obviously impracticable for her to keep on the lease of Summerhill indefinitely so Linger was charged with the task of finding a suitable winter residence to be turned into a sort of Irish Gödollo.

Apart from social chatter which was bound to bring the news back to them, the Irish Special Branch of the English intelligence service was at that time exceedingly efficient and the Marlboroughs heard of her intentions almost immediately. They were still smarting under Parnell's attack ('Whenever you saw a Raw, rub it,' was one of the Four Gospels he laid down to be followed by another Irish politician and right well he himself obeyed it), and this on top of it was altogether too much. If Parnell was the uncrowned King of Ireland, as he boasted himself with some truth to be, she, if she were to return, would surely do so as the uncrowned Queen.

Reports went back to London that the course she contemplated was quite unthinkable and could not be tolerated. At last diplomatic wires began to hum.

Franz Joseph was just then in the throes of grappling with the changes in foreign policy that Taaffe, Andrassy's successor, was attempting to initiate. The foreign policy of the Empire was changing and being redirected. Although at first sight England did not seem to be in any way concerned with these changes there was always the possibility that she could or would interest herself in them to the Empire's detriment. Above all, at that juncture, the Emperor wanted an accommodation with Russia. But if Russia made her western flank secure she would be free to turn her eyes and her armies to the East. England was always suspicious of Russian designs on India and fearful of an invasion across the North-West frontier. A generation before, Lord John Russell had summed up British policy towards Russian aims in the East in one brief sentence: 'If we do not stop Russia on the Danube, we shall have to stop her on the Indus.'

The last thing which Franz Joseph wanted at that moment was a dispute with any nation, let alone one as strong and powerful as Great Britain. Now it was suddenly brought to his attention that his wife's activities in Ireland, innocent though they appeared to be, were causing grave embarrassment to the English government and what amounted to hostility in the Court of St James's. Where the security of his Empire and his dynasty was concerned Franz Joseph was prepared to act with decision and ruthlessness, even if such action interfered with his darling Sisi's pleasures and happiness. He issued immediate instructions to her to return forthwith.

It can only be imagined how she received this dashing of her hopes. But she obeyed. She, too, by now must have realised that when Franz Joseph was driven to the lengths of actually giving her orders, he meant what he said. Without stating any reason for her decision she announced that she was cutting short her visit and returning to Vienna. But before she left she had one other call to pay and this was an appointment she was determined to keep.

Henry Eyre Linde, of Eyrefield Lodge, The Curragh, was the most famous trainer of steeplechasers of his day. He had had a colourful career commencing as a constable in the Royal Irish Constabulary. Even there he soon showed he had something approaching genius in the management and care of horses. When he married a woman of some means he left the police, bought what was said to have once been his ancestral home and began a career of unrivalled success as a trainer. From Eyrefield Lodge he sent out a constant stream of winners not only in Ireland and England but all over the Continent, too, which was virtually unheard of in those days of slow and difficult transport. Brutally outspoken and no respecter of persons, he never lost the roughness of tongue he had acquired in the constabulary or his pronounced Irish brogue. 'His nationality was never mistaken whether it was at Aintree or Auteuil', one writer said of him, and it might be added that his presence never went unnoticed, either, for his opinions were expressed in forthright and ringing terms that had been known to carry clear across the Curragh in a high wind. His establishment was said to be as rough and ready as himself but he was a great stableman and his horses lacked for nothing, nor did they ever leave Eyrefield Lodge short of schooling. He had a steeplechase course built in his grounds and, in the brothers Beasley, the most superb schooling jockeys and best riders in the three kingdoms. He had been presented to the Empress when she hunted with the Kildare and had issued an invitation to her to visit Eyrefield Lodge and see the horses.

This she was quite determined to do and on the day before she left she, Middleton and Rudi Liechtenstein took a special train to Newbridge and then drove over to Eyrefield Lodge.

Linde had been warned to watch his language. He was on his best behaviour and at first all went well. The Empress was entranced, as she always was with blood horses, and she, too, was at her most charming and gracious and looked her loveliest. Linde was bewitched immediately. He insisted on bringing her to see Tommy Beasley schooling the young horses over the steeplechase course, a privilege granted to only the very select few. One of these youngsters especially caught her eye. Linde explained that he had done very little with him and he doubted if he would jump the course without a fall. But, under the skilled and careful hands of Beasley, he went round twice without the semblance of a mistake. The Empress was delighted. As the horse pulled up she clapped her hands together and exclaimed: 'This is too good!' Whereupon Linde bowed and swept off his hat. 'Your Majesty,' he said, 'in honour of you and this visit I shall name him Toogood.' And he did.

The Empress, as usual where horses were concerned, had shown good judgement. Running in the colours of the Hungarian Count Erdody, Toogood won the Grand Steeplechase de Paris in 1883 and Linde telegraphed the news to Vienna immediately he passed the post. It has been suggested that Middleton later returned to Eyrefield Lodge and bought him for her and that Count Erdody was merely her nominee. This may or may not be true. Toogood was a good horse and was second in the Grand National of 1886. But, like most things she touched, if she did touch him, he was unlucky, for he was plagued by leg trouble and never quite fulfilled his early promise. Linde had another surprise for her. He had in his stable a brilliant and most handsome chestnut mare of whom he thought the world. She was a mare of great charm and presence. It was said of her that everyone who saw her fell in love with her on the spot, so it was entirely appropriate that Linde should have named her Empress in honour of his visitor.

The trainer escorted the party along the boxes examining their inmates as they went until they came to where Empress was housed. Linde had prepared a pretty speech. 'Now, Your Majesty,' he said, bowing low, 'I will show you the winner of the Liverpool this year. She is the most beautiful mare I have ever had in my care and I have named her Empress in honour of the most beautiful and charming lady ever to grace my humble establishment.'

The door was then opened with a flourish. Linde bowed again and everyone crowded round. Unfortunately, the principal actress in the little scene seemed determined to take no part in it. Quite impervious to the honour that was being done to her and the attentions of her Imperial visitor she was lying down in the box with her back to the party. And, what is more, she showed no signs of getting to her feet despite the opening of the door and the unaccustomed movements of strangers near her. Warnings of imminent approach of thunder which his stable lads knew only too well, began to appear on Linde's brow.

He entered the box and still the mare remained lying down. His whole carefully prepared tableau was in the process of being ruined. The rumbling of approaching thunder became more apparent and the head lad, who was with the party, thought it convenient to take himself elsewhere. Advancing further into the box the trainer approached the mare and told her in tones stern but moderately muted to get to her feet. She raised her head, looked at him—and remained where she was.

At this, fury and disappointment possessed Linde and the storm broke. Proprieties, guest and everything else forgotten, he took two steps forward. Then he drew back his foot and administered the mare a hefty kick in the ribs, at the same time roaring at her the words that have passed into lore on the Curragh: 'Get up, you bitch!'

Fortunately, one of the lace handkerchiefs was at hand in which the Empress could bury her face as she sought to conceal her laughter. Linde, horrified at what he had done, was the next moment covered in the utmost confusion. He need not have been. Had he known her at all he would have realised that she liked men to be themselves and would have far preferred him thus, acting naturally, than in his unaccustomed stiff and ceremonial manner of the earlier part of the visit. He was right about the mare, too, just as she had been about the horse. Empress did win the National a few weeks later, ridden by Tommy Beasley and with a ton of money on her, some of which may well have been Middleton's—and Elizabeth's, for all we know.

After that there came the business of departure. Gifts were made to all the household, MacDonald and Tom Healy being especially honoured. Mrs Davis, wife of Langford's agent, was presented with an enormous Austrian greyhound 'measuring from his hind feet to the tip of his nose six feet seven and a half inches'. Morrogh received a diamond stock pin and her grateful thanks for all the superb sport he had shown her. Linger, her secretary, was told to arrange for a large sum to be donated to the Lord Mayor of Dublin to alleviate distress amongst the poor of the city.

The Marlboroughs were determined to prevent any 'disloyal' demonstration taking place at her departure and this time her train went straight through to the quayside at North Wall without stopping in Dublin. No one was allowed on to the platform without special permission. The crowds who had come to cheer her were dispersed to reassemble as best they could some distance away along the quays. Lord Crofton and Colonel Forster were there to represent the authorities and to take formal leave of her. Captain Middleton and Lord Langford were the only other persons present.

It was the SS *Shamrock* once again that was waiting for her. In defiance of convention, incognito and official ukases, it proudly flew the Austrian Imperial ensign as she went on board. Then, with the minimum of ceremony, it cast off and bore her away down the Liffey to the open sea, leaving for the last time and forever the country she had loved so much. The Irish people had returned her love with affection, recognition and respect. The crowds lining the quays cheered and cheered again as the steamer slowly vanished into the evening mists.

Another hope of happiness had been dashed. She stood for a little while in the stern of the *Shamrock*, a lonely figure with the seawind whipping her veil about her, gazing back at the green hills and blue mountains behind Dublin. Then she raised her hand in a gesture, part resignation, part salutation. Solitary on the quayside, standing apart from the rest of the little official gathering, a man raised a hand in response. Then she went below. Middleton, for it was he who had waited, turned and made his way to where Langford and a carriage stood ready to bring him back to Summerhill.

By three o'clock the next afternoon she was at Paddington. On this occasion there was to be no avoiding the visits and meetings incumbent upon royalty. Franz Joseph had laid it down that the courtesies must be obeyed and in this instance she realised that he intended his instructions to be followed.

Privately she might write to her mother that the whole thing 'bored her terribly' but, like many another wife who has lost her love for a forceful husband yet remained married to him, she had kept, at least to some degree, her awe of him. Especially was this the case when he addressed himself to her in one of his moods of majesty and with all the panoply of Empire behind him.

The Prince of Wales met her at the station and drove with her to Claridge's. There had been some talk of Rudolph joining her in London and the Prince giving a ball for them both. Rudolph, however, was in Brussels, at the end of a tour of Europe in search of a suitable wife, sufficiently Catholic and well-bred to carry the onus and responsibility of becoming, in time, an empress. Elizabeth knew nothing of his travels or their object, only that he had arrived in Belgium and was remaining there and so, to her great relief, the ball was abandoned.

The following morning she paid an early visit to the Prince and Princess of Wales at Marlborough House and made a special request to be shown the stables, then said to be one of the most modern in Europe. She was in no hurry to pay her respects to Queen Victoria and, in private, some court officials doubted if the visit would take place at all. But the Queen had returned from Buckingham Palace to Windsor with the express purpose of receiving her there, so, despite her reluctance, she had little alternative but to go.

She left her departure from London as late in the morning as possible and kept the duration of her visit to the shortest time consistent with protocol and courtesy. She is said to have been noticeably bored throughout and the Queen to have been at her most regal and frigid. If this was so the Queen recorded none of it in her diary and instead remarked upon the graciousness and natural manner of her guest. The Empress may indeed, with characteristic unpredictability, have at the last moment decided to be charming and, if she did, even the old Queen, disapproving as she was of her attitudes and activities, could not entirely resist her.

Later that evening, on her return from Windsor, she met Disraeli, who in turn charmed and amused her and then she dined privately with the Karolyis. But around midday the next morning a telegram was handed to her. As she read it she turned pale and uttered a gasp. Countess Festetics, who was with her at the time, enquired anxiously if the telegram had brought terrible news.

'The Crown Prince is betrothed to Princess Stephanie,' was the reply. Wrapped up in her own concerns, in her hunting and her happiness in Ireland, she had known nothing of the Emperor's plans for securing the succession and the dynasty through a suitable Catholic marriage.

'Thank God', the Countess said, 'that it is not the news of some disaster.'

'Heaven send that it be not one,' was the Empress' reply.

Her forebodings and intuition in this instance were, of course, both true and accurate. Whenever she gave herself the time to think about him she knew her son's character better than anyone, even perhaps than he did himself.

Rudolph was a great lover of women. But he liked them svelte and smart, witty and beautiful. Now he was betrothed to one whom her own uncle described as having all the daintiness of a dragoon and whose voice an acquaintance referred to as 'closely resembling the fog-horn of a Danube tug-boat'.

The Empress broke her journey home in Brussels and what she saw of Stephanie there did not reassure her. 'The Empress', Count Lonyay wrote long afterwards, 'thought only in horse terms. Never would it have occurred to the Master of the Horse of the Imperial Court to harness a racehorse and an Irish hunter to the same carriage, yet, without so much as a thought, Rudolph's parents allowed their over-bred son to be tied to the thick-boned Belgian.'

This is unfair to the Empress, who had no say in the matter and was noticeably concerned and worried by the approaching marriage. For once she sought solace from Franz Joseph, constantly repeating that she hoped it would turn out all right, only to be met with the brusque assurance that of course it would and that she worried too much.

She was terribly depressed and in low spirits all that spring and summer. In an attempt to cheer herself up and to recapture at least some of the lost happiness of her time in Ireland she commissioned Richter, the famous Viennese horse-painter, to make portraits of the hunters which she had brought back with her: Domino, Hard Times, The Doctor, Summerhill, Ashtown,

Cameo and St Patrick, they were each of them painted and hung in a special room in the Hofburg which she called her riding chapel. She spent hours there gazing at the paintings while she sought to re-live again the pleasure and excitement they had given her, the gay Irish atmosphere and the companionship of Captain Middleton.

Richter's fee was enormous, as was the cost of this second Irish visit. When the figures for the purchase of the additional horses, their movement and transport to and from Ireland, together with her travel by special boat and train and that of the myriads of servants, the suite and the rest of the retinue came in the final total was staggering.

It is perhaps no wonder that Franz Joseph, considering the account when it was placed before him for authorisation, let the mask slip for once. He initialled the direction for payment of.the huge sum but he pencilled in the margin the words: 'If only you had never seen a saddle.'

CHAPTER NINE

Cheshire

In England, almost immediately after her departure, on 8 March to be precise, Disraeli prorogued Parliament and called a snap election. Gladstone had been stumping the country for weeks prior to prorogation making impassioned electioneering speeches with the energy of a man thirty years his junior. Disraeli's gamble failed. The Whigs came back and with them, despite the opposition of the Queen, 'that *half-mad fire-brand* who would soon ruin everything and be a *Dictator*.'

Gladstone was duly installed as Prime Minister and with him into office came his friend Lord Spencer. Spencer, however, was not then given the Viceroyalty of Ireland, the prize he must have hoped for; but was instead made Lord President of the Council. Even before the election Marlborough had asked to be relieved of his post. Cowper, a nonentity with all the social graces, was sent to Ireland to try to keep the landlords and gentry in hand and to allay their fears of confiscation and revolution.

Gladstone was determined to come to grips with the Irish problem: to relieve distress, introduce tenant-right and even, as it transpired, to sponsor some measure of Home Rule. His policies of alleviation, meagre though at first they were, foundered in the Lords.

The west of Ireland erupted into violence and what was virtually an open land war. In June, one of the Land League leaders was advising tenants: 'If you have no way of getting a rifle, sell the old cow and buy one.' In September came the farcical but far-reaching incident of Captain Boycott and his rents. By November Cowper was writing hysterically to Gladstone that 'something like a general massace of all landowners and agents not under police protection is a conceivable and possible event'.

Parnell's position as uncrowned king of Ireland was enormously strengthened by the breakdown of the usual channels of administration, and the fact that the people were now looking to the Land League and not the law to redress their grievances. Moreover, by controlling in Parliament the sixty votes of the Irish members, he spoke and acted from a position where he could materially influence the issue of events.

All these things, of course, quite passed the Empress by. Since she was no longer interested in the politics of her own country it was unlikely that she would remotely concern herself with the internal affairs of another. As Rudolph wrote to Latour in December of that year: 'There was a time when the Empress was interested in politics, how effectively I am unable to say . . . These times have passed. The august lady is now only interested in sport.'

Rudolph was absolutely right. But Irish politics were to have a compelling influence on her plans, her future and her hopes of happiness nonetheless.

For, above all, she wanted to return to Ireland. Lord Langford, who visited her in the autumn, appears to have attempted to reassure both her and the Emperor that a visit in the spring would be perfectly feasible. He brought with him, too, other and more disturbing news. Bay Middleton had had a terrible fall at Towcester. He had struck his head against the iron park railings that bordered the course. There were then no skull caps or protective helmets and riders only wore the thin silk of their racing caps to protect their heads. He had suffered a serious fracture of the skull and was lying unconscious. She was miserable and inconsolable until the news was brought that he had recovered consciousness and was beginning to regain his health. His tremendous strength and vitality soon fought off the effects of the injury. After a month or so he was back in the saddle again and going as bravely as ever. She received a message which must have gladdened her heart that he was willing and ready to pilot her once more at the top of the hunt over any country in the world should she come back.

Ireland was the place she chose for their reunion. Lord Langford had told her no harm would befall her there and further reassurance was at hand, too, though from an unlikely quarter. It appears that Parnell had conveyed to her, unofficially, though it may well have been through Karolyi or someone at the Embassy—young Charles Kinsky had just taken up an appointment there and Karolyi's staff was always thronged with Hungarian hunting and racing men—that he, personally, would see to her sport and her safety. Despite all this the Emperor, having considered the matter and remembering the bad feeling engendered by the previous visit, placed an absolute veto on any suggestion of a return.

This interference with her ambitions was not taken with the best of pleasure by the Empress. Negotiations had already been started to secure an Irish residence. Since Summerhill was no longer available, Kilkenny Castle was suggested as an alternative. Its vast size would easily house the entire retinue and Chicken Hartopp had just taken over the Kilkenny Hounds. By a mixture of bravery, effrontery, eccentricity and panache, he had gained the affection of the countryside and, despite the disturbances, was showing wonderful sport.

Elizabeth consoled herself and those who had eagerly awaited her return by sending Richter's portrait of herself on Domino as a present to Leonard Morrogh. Once again the gift went slightly awry. The picture was addressed to the Ward Hunt Kennels. The hunt committee, thinking it a present to themselves, appropriated it. Morrogh claimed it as his and another wrangle ensued. The committee refused to part with the picture and it hangs in the committee-room to this day, though the fence she is shown to be jumping bears little resemblance to anything she would have been likely to encounter in the Meath or Ward countries.

Even if Ireland were barred to her, she was nevertheless determined to hunt with Middleton again. The unhappy memories of her last visit to the Pytchley were with her still so she would not countenance a return to the Shires. An alternative was not easy to find for not every country contained a mansion empty, available and sufficiently large to contain horses, suite and servants.

Combermere Abbey in Cheshire was where the choice finally fell and a curious story circulated as to how it came to be selected.

Sir Watkin Williams-Wynn was the greatest landowner and magnate in North Wales. He kept a private pack of hounds which he hunted over his own immense property. This stretched through Denbighshire and Flintshire and into Cheshire and Shropshire. So great were his holdings and the style he kept up that he was known as 'The Prince in Wales'. Many years before, or so it was said, he had employed a Hungarian cook. Clever, ambitious and thrifty, this young man contrived to save sufficient money to return to his native country as a man of means. There he entered the Empress's service where his brains and ability gained him swift advancement. He was Herr Linger, her private secretary.

When the Irish visit fell through, Linger wrote to his old master explaining the difficulties he was having in finding for the Empress another hunting centre with a suitable residence. Lord Combermere was visiting Wynnstay Park at the time the letter arrived, and it was discussed between them. Combermere told his host that he proposed going to the West Indies to see his property there after Christmas and that the Abbey would be vacant. Linger was apprised of this, negotiations were put in train and an agreement was reached that the Empress should take the Abbey for the latter part of February and the month of March at a rent of £600 per month. Austrian officials were sent over in a hurry to carry out the necessary improvements and alterations, the chief of which was the installation of a chapel and a gymnasium and the wiring of the whole house with electric bells for Her Majesty's use. They also arranged for the construction of an additional waiting room at Wrenbury, the little wayside station which served the Abbey, since she would be using it extensively when taking the many specials required for her hunting expeditions. A new siding was also put down, to accommodate the railway horse-boxes for her and her party. All this cost the Emperor the nice round sum of £10,000.

And then, at the last moment, it appeared that the whole thing might be cancelled and none of these expensive alterations used at all. For, suddenly, there seemed the possibility of a reprieve and that another visit to Ireland could take place.

Parnell had by no means given up the idea of welcoming in person a foreign Catholic sovereign to his native land and of showing the English how he could protect and serve one who was truly loved and admired. It was a splendid opportunity to rub a raw spot even rawer. Late in January he and certain members of his party called on Count Karolyi. They requested him to present a memorial to the Empress on their behalf, telling Her Majesty how quiet Ireland was, that there was no reason why she should not come to hunt there and they promised her a hearty welcome.

Karolyi knew how much the Empress longed to return to Ireland but he also knew that this was not the proper way of going about it. He appears privately to have let the Empress know what was happening and thus set her spirits soaring, but in his official capacity he did what he had to do as Ambassador. He formally told the Foreign Secretary, Granville, of the request, adding that the action he proposed to take was to inform Parnell that he was not the proper channel of communication and that he ought to address himself in such matters to Sir H. Elliot, Her Majesty's Ambassador to Austria.

Granville, knowing the strength of the feeling caused by her last visit to Ireland, was horrified when he heard of the approach. He immediately wrote back to Karolyi in the stiffest terms stating that 'The first part of his (Karolyi's) answer would be sufficient, that with reference to so extraordinary a document it was not his (Karolyi's) business to point out to Irish Homerulers the channels through which they might address the Empress.'

Karolyi wrote back equally stiffly saying that he had returned the memorial, but nothing more. Then Granville sent off the entire correspondence to the Queen pointing out that although Karolyi had returned the memorial he had, nevertheless, given no indication of how he himself was going to deal with the request. Whereupon the Queen's pent-up resentment about Parnell, Ireland and the Empress, and everything connected with them, exploded on to paper:

> Osborne 9 Jan 1881
>
> The Queen has received Lord Granville's letter giving an account of the conduct of the 'Pretender Parnell' (for such he is), with respect to the Empress of Austria with amazement. It is *rather* too much! Lord Granville's answer was quite right. But he should let Sir H. Elliot know of it—and

the Emperor should be warned of such a proceeding.

The Emperor was indeed warned, and in no uncertain terms, and Elizabeth's hopes were dashed again. The omens were not auspicious for her first visit to Cheshire.

Nevertheless, when she arrived at Wrenbury on the evening of 15 February, having travelled clear across England without pausing for any state visits or salutations, she appeared in good spirits enough. Bay Middleton was waiting for her on the platform and her first words to him after enquiring for his health were: 'How are the horses?'

The answer was that the horses were indeed well. Bayzand had retired and MacDonald and Tom Healy had charge of them. They had brought across from Ireland the four Austrian horses they had been schooling there and these, with the rest of the string, made the number ready for her up to twelve.

Rudi Liechtenstein had eight and Tom Healy, now fully promoted to 'rider in attendance', six, some of which were, however, to be reserved for Her Majesty. These filled the Combermere stables to capacity and Middleton's string of ten had to find quarters a mile or so away at Burley Dam.

She had brought with her a larger personal suite than had attended her in Ireland. Countess Festetics, Johann and Heinrich Larisch, Rudi Liechtenstein and Middleton, all had rooms in the Abbey. Marie Larisch was back in favour but she and Georg had to find temporary quarters at Whitchurch, as had young Charles Kinsky, then attached to the Austrian Embassy. He was, however, given leave to join the Imperial entourage for the first time and was tremendously excited about it all.

Her good mood did not last and the hoped-for happiness did not return. The Abbey itself was comfortable enough. It was picturesque, wild and romantic—all things she loved. The first Lord Combermere had been Stapleton Cotton, Wellington's Peninsular cavalry commander, but the Abbey had been in the family since Henry VIII gave it to a Cotton on the dissolution of the monasteries. She had a suite of sitting room, bedroom, bathroom, gymnasium and chapel, a special room for her dresses and a waiting room for her attendants. The sitting room had a bay window with a vista looking out over the woods and the lake. A special staircase had been constructed from it leading down to her own kitchen so that meals could be served privately there when she wished.

This was all very well and she could laugh at Countess Festetics who was installed in the room where William of Orange had slept in 1682. The Countess disliked the faded orange wallpaper put up in his honour and unchanged since and was afraid of falling out of his high bed.

But the hunting was not at all to Elizabeth's liking. She had been told that the Cheshire country resembled Ireland. It was true that it was fenced with banks and ditches but there she found the resemblance ended, at least compared with Meath and Kildare, the galloping countries she had loved so much. Here both the enclosures and the fences were small. The result was a trappy, scrambling sort of country which suited neither herself nor her horses. She wanted to gallop and jump, to encounter danger when her blood was up and hounds were flying. Most of her horses were of the type best suited to provide this excitement and Cameo, in particular, always a tricky ride in a trappy country, disliked Cheshire almost as much as she did herself. In fact, she found that with the exception of Hard Times, an old favourite, the Austrian horses left behind in Ireland and carefully schooled by MacDonald and Healy, went best for her in this new and different country.

It was Middleton once more who came to her rescue and restored her spirits. He pointed out that this new country was only a fresh challenge to her horsemanship and went on to say that with him as her pilot he knew she could meet it and surmount it. This was just the spur she needed and forthwith she set about showing the way in Cheshire as she had done everywhere else.

Middleton, as always, was both devoted and attentive. He, too, was determined to demonstrate that he could pilot her as brilliantly here as elsewhere and that he had lost none of his skill and dash since his accident. His reputation had, of course, preceded him. He meant to live up to it and he did.

The first day the Imperial party came out was a special bye-day put on for them at the South Cheshire kennels at Adderley. Only a dozen people had been told of the meet. Most of them were Cheshire thrusters. One of these, looking at Middleton, the stranger from the Shires with the tall reputation, asked Charles Kinsky how good he really was. 'If you want to find out,' was the answer, 'follow him—if you can.'

It was Middleton's presence, his way with her and her horses, that persuaded her to stay on and to try to enjoy herself. It was not the same as those wonderful days in Ireland—nothing ever could be—but gradually she came to accept it as a substitute, a second best and a fairly good one. The horses, too, commenced to acclimatise themselves and three of them, Quicksilver, Sunflower and the quaintly named Butterduck, were turning out really well. In all, during the visit she had twenty-two days hunting out of a possible twenty-eight, of which two were lost through snow. On each of these days save two, when he was away racing, Middleton piloted her. In his absence the honour fell on Major Rivers-Bulkeley, a Cheshire man whom Moreton Frewen recalled as 'a square-shouldered rider and not particularly "fashionable" to look at on a horse; but he rode all sorts and conditions of horses equally well'.

One of Bay's absences racing was to attend the Fair Oaks Meeting at Birmingham. The National Hunt Steeplechase was held there that year and again he had an unsuccessful attempt at winning it. His mount, Bowsprit, fell on the flat bringing down another horse which rolled over him. He was knocked out for a few minutes and carried back to the weighing-room unconscious.

The Empress was worried, anxious and attentive when she heard of the fall and he was noticeably quiet that evening at dinner. But he insisted on coming out next day to pilot her with Sir Watkin Wynn's at Clovery. He brought her through a big crowd riding hard 'for the honour of Shropshire' with his usual flair for the right line to take and the right place to pick. They were there together when hounds rolled their fox over in the open and Charles Payne, the huntsman, presented her with the brush. It is to be wondered at that he occupied a special place in her heart?

Marie Larisch was duly displaying over the Cheshire country the one talent she had which had nothing of duplicity about it—that of riding a horse brilliantly, to hounds or anywhere else. By this she was winning her way firmly back into the Empress's affections. She was much at Combermere and more and more became a confidante. This increased the envy and jealousy of Countess Festetics, who could not follow her into the hunting field.

Countess Larisch says that Middleton was constantly alone in the Empress's apartments when they were not hunting. This may or may not be true. Certainly other old friends came along to pay their respects. Langford was down for several days, and Spencer tore himself away from his Parliamentary duties to enjoy a day's hunting in her company with the North Shropshire at Hawstone Hill.

Yet, despite all these compensations, things were not the same as they had been and she knew it. Whatever Middleton or anyone else said, the country could not rival the elusive charm of Ireland and the Irish which had so laid its hand upon her. The sense of apartness, feyness and the strange excitements of Ireland were lacking here and she sadly missed them. Then, too, rumours and whispers were carried back to her that the Baird family were becoming restive at Middleton's continued neglect of their sister and the fact that everywhere his name was linked with hers. The Baird influence in the world of hunting and racing was steadily increasing. Charlotte's brother had taken over the Mastership of the Cottesmore the previous year, another brother was shortly to be elected a member of the Jockey Club, while their kinsman, the raffish millionaire Abingdon Baird, was riding winners everywhere and had not yet incurred the warning-off sentence which was to drive him to dissipation and ruin. These were men whose hostility it was better to avoid and both he and she must have known it.

All her life she hated letting anyone go. An attachment to her was to be maintained forever, or until she decided to break it. The thought of losing him must have been torture to her. Yet now, at last, that nine years' difference in age was beginning to tell. She had reached her forty-third year and, fit, active and determined though she was, the effort of keeping up with him in front of fields all out for glory, honour and reputation, through twenty-two consecutive days hunting, broken only by brief rests on Sundays, brought with it its own physical toll. She was driving herself too hard and with over-tiredness came restlessness and inability to sleep. These in their train brought with them the terror that they might cause her to lose her looks and her figure. To combat this threat came ever more frequent and lengthy sessions in front of her glass, scanning her lovely features and wonderful complexion for the faintest beginnings of telltale wrinkles or blemishes. Secret and elaborate recipes to guard and preserve beauty were sent for from Austria. When she was not riding she was walking or exercising in the improvised gymnasium to keep her muscles taut and trim. Lest the first hint of a spreading waist should even begin to show she refused to eat normal meals. Turtles were sent for to cater to her love of a special turtle soup. The remainder of her diet consisted for the most part of meat juice, much of it raw, and fruit. The nightly hair-dressing ritual with Frau von Feyfalik became longer and more intense. She was still immensely proud of her wonderful auburn tresses and that they reached, when loosed, to her waist and beyond. Both she and the dresser scrutinised them with the exactitude born of nervous worry for the first betraying flecks of grey.

All this wasting and worrying and burning up of highly strung energy had a disastrous effect on her nerves. For the first time her immediate and intimate circle found her becoming almost irritable with them, though it was noticeable that Middleton was excepted from the angry outbursts when they came. She was in no state to withstand the inevitable worldly irritations that, as ever, began to accumulate about her.

North Wales had an overwhelming non-conformist population, then given to the very strictest Sunday observance. At best they did not much approve of the presence amongst them of a foreign Catholic monarch who had Popish Masses celebrated in her private chapel at Combermere every Sunday and saint's day. When the rumour began to circulate that she had draghounds out in Combermere Park after Mass on Sunday, local indignation ran high. A report of the alleged occurrence and a protest appeared in a newspaper circulating in the locality. It was, of course, entirely inaccurate for no such event had taken place and a denial was promptly issued by Linger. What she had done was to follow her usual practice and have Tom Healy erect schooling fences in the park over which she rode her horses to get them jumping just as she wanted. She also used these fences to try out prospective purchases for, as she said in a letter to Ida Ferenczy, 'everyone here wants to sell me a horse'.

Tom Healy used them, too, for schooling and trying out horses. Since she was hunting every other day Sunday was the only day when this could be done but it must be said that it was scarcely a tactful day to choose in that non-conformist country, though it would never have occurred to her to consider the wisdom or otherwise of what she proposed to do.

That small episode upset her and then it was brought to her notice that the Austrian public and press were beginning to express more openly and strongly their disapproval of her long absences and their purposes. Correspondence concerning her hunting activities was appearing in the left-wing press. Indeed, letters in this vein addressed directly to her were arriving at Combermere. One of them, which was couched in the roughest terms, asking for an advance of the cost of one day's hunting in England so that the writer could carry on his business and avoid bankruptcy caused her the gravest offence. Then Nopsca, on a visit to London, found an article in an English socialist weekly attacking her and her activities. With an uncharacteristic lack of tact he brought the article back to Combermere with him and showed it to her and she was greatly upset. She wrote:

My dear Ida,

Sunday—It is now a week since I put aside the letter I had begun since Marie arrived and we began to gossip until luncheon . . . I received the attached article from Nopsca yesterday. He brought it from London and is extremely sorry about it. You will be equally angry when Nopsca has time to translate it for you. He and I are by now used to this sort of thing. I should be very surprised now if anyone spoke well of me . . . I tried out a horse I received today from Ireland. I galloped and jumped him a great deal.

I embrace you and send you greetings,

ERZEBET

But despite her depressions and wayward moods she still retained her power to fascinate. Georg Larisch, Marie's husband, who had at first been deeply resentful of her influence over his wife, saw much of her at that time. Marie and he were constantly summoned from Whitchurch to Combermere,

Marie for a gossip or, as Marie herself implies, to play the part of a compliant chaperone, while Georg looked over the horses or helped Tom Healy school them. Out hunting Georg watched the Empress and Middleton sailing away in front of them all, and felt his admiration for her steadily growing. Soon his resentment was converted into a willing adulation. He became and remained an ardent admirer, even if he was never quite admitted into the little band that formed her innermost circle. One who is still alive and who had heard men who knew her at that time tell of her and her doings has written: 'When they spoke of her it was in a way I have never heard anyone spoken of —even their voices took on a special timbre . . .' No wonder Middleton remained entranced and that, despite the pressures upon him, he could not bring himself to leave her side.

It was Middleton who was her chosen companion when they journeyed from Wrenbury to Aintree to see the Grand National. There was a great gathering of friends for the occasion since Langford and Colonel Forster had come over from Ireland to join the party. Kinsky, too, was in the special train, along with the inevitable Rudi Liechtenstein, but it was Middleton who escorted her along the platform at Edgehill station with the rest of the suite following behind. Lord Sefton had put a private brougham at her disposal. They entered it together and were driven to the course.

The weather was terrible. It rained and blew all day and the race was run in a rainstorm. She did, however, have the pleasure of seeing yet another of Linde's horses, Woodbrook, ridden by Tommy Beasley, who had ridden Empress the year before, win the great race. Afterwards she made sure the trainer was presented to her and they renewed old acquaintance. She was happier and more at home with him than when she made her formal courtesy calls on the Grosvenors at Eaton Hall and Sir Watkin Williams-Wynn at Wynnstay Park. These were followed by a brief and chilling interview with Queen Victoria at Buckingham Palace when she broke her return journey in London.

Then the special steamer *Maid of Kent* bore her back again to the middle-European world she hated so much and to all the stresses and complications that were to arise from Rudolph's wedding.

CHAPTER TEN

Renunciation

Rudolph's marriage was a misalliance in every sense of the word, and his mother knew it. His bride, Princess Stephanie of Belgium, was a homely, immature, tactless frump, who would have been far better as a Flemish *hausfrau* than as the wife of the heir-apparent of the Austrian throne. Rudolph himself was difficult, diseased and highly intelligent. He was also at that time much under the influence of a brilliant editor and journalist of left-wing ideas, Maurice Szeps, the founder of *Neues Weiner Tageblatt*. At the time of the marriage the extraordinary situation had arisen in which Rudolph was anonymously writing leaders for Szeps's paper advocating liberal ideas and attacking the hidebound and reactionary attitudes of the aristocracy. He still retained his intense dislike for arrogant and caste-conscious men such as Middleton and Kinsky. One of his most famous articles was entitled *Noble Window Smashers*, which contained a telling and vitriolic attack on a group of young bloods who had just broken up the house of a prominent jew. It was just the sort of cruel prank that men like Middleton and Kinsky could, and indeed did, get up to, for jew-baiting was a universal sport of the upper classes until Edward VII made it both unpopular and unfashionable. The article was shot through with such bitterness as to make it seem almost a personal attack and Szeps had to water it down before publication. Rudolph was never to forget the humiliations he had received at the hands of his mother's high-born and horse-minded friends.

There were others, too, of an unforgetting nature. Count Lonyay says that Queen Victoria refused to give official permission for the Prince of Wales to attend Rudolph's wedding, ostensibly because she disapproved of Rudolph's reckless way of life. He quotes Baron Mitis as his authority for this. If she did take such a step, it seems far more likely that she was still full of resentment at Elizabeth's attempt to come to Ireland and allow 'Pretender' Parnell another opportunity of rubbing a raw spot.

In fact, the Prince did attend the wedding, though the manner of his attendance was sufficiently unusual to cause comment. He travelled without the Princess and stayed, not at a royal house, but at an hotel. The reason he gave was that he wished to meet certain members of the Austrian branch of Rothschilds, a family who, being Jews and commoners, the Emperor did not recognise at all. The Prince's visit for the wedding was carried out in a singularly off-hand way which was most unlike him for on these occasions he was usually a stickler for protocol. The fact of the matter was, of course, that relations between the two royal houses were just then extremely strained and Sisi and Middleton with their love for hunting and each other were the highly unlikely cause of it all.

None of this had any effect on Elizabeth's intention to return for another season in England. Personalities mattered to her, not politics, and it was another marriage now which was giving her cause for concern. This was Middleton's, which was looming nearer and nearer, though no date had as yet been fixed. It was unlikely that she would have admitted it, even to herself, but it does seem certain that, at least subconsciously, she meant to prevent this marriage if she could. As with all her inner circle there was a bond that bound him to her and this must not be broken. She had prevented the proposed marriage of Countess Festetics and had seen to it that Ida Ferenczy remained faithful only to her. Rudi Liechtenstein's permanent bachelordom was accepted as a tribute to his undying and hopeless worship at the shrine of her beauty; the young Charles Kinsky, the latest acolyte, did not marry until years after her death and then not entirely happily. It was unthinkable that the closest and dearest of them all should break the fetters. Besides, she now fully realised that hunting in England constituted her only escape from boredom and the nervous afflictions which came with it. There was no time to be bored when hounds were running and the only problem to be faced was the physical one of successfully surmounting the next fence. And hunting without him was unthinkable. Apart altogether from the sport and success he brought her, in her intensely feminine way she loved the domination he exerted over her when they hunted together. The shouts of where and when to go, the uninhibited language when she disobeyed, redeemed always by his infectious laugh, were things to be treasured and preserved. Then, too, there was the immense vitality of the man which seemed to emanate into something almost tangible about him and which inspired her to feats she knew even she could not have achieved without him. He made her reputation whilst maintaining his own, just as she, from her presence and position, made him play a part, a minor one perhaps, but still a part, in the histories of the two great Empires that then dominated Europe and the world.

For five seasons now they had ridden and hunted together, discussed horseflesh, what to try and what to buy, what to discard and what to keep, how to ride one horse or another, and plotted out a hunting programme. She was unlikely to give all this up without a struggle. And in this struggle she would have the enormous advantage of beauty, position, wealth and power.

Others appreciated all this, too. In her absence the pressures on Middleton mounted. The engagement had gone on long enough. He must now either declare a day or release the girl. Here again the code came in: he was a gentleman; the latter alternative was unthinkable; he had given his word and would keep it. These were imponderables which Elizabeth would have been unlikely to have taken into account or to have understood if she did.

Middleton came up to scratch and a day was named. It was, however, still a long way off, for the month was to be October and much could happen in the intervening time. But for Middleton, nevertheless, the date having been made definite, it was clear also that the rest of the code must be observed and that his association with the Empress must cease. When she arrived in England in the first week of February, the shattering news awaited her that he would no longer be available to pilot her. The choice of a substitute fell on Major Rivers-Bulkeley who was embarrassed by the honour thrust upon him and did not know quite how to cope with it.

Just as she had always done, she was out hunting a day after her arrival. But, despite the fact that the old familiar faces were all about her, Liechtenstein, Heinrich Larisch and Tom Healy, and that the young Larischs were expected to arrive at Whitchurch any day, nothing could compensate for Bay's absence.

Major Rivers-Bulkeley, a man of quiet and retiring disposition, did not feel that he could address an empress with direct instructions in the hunting field. He was therefore puzzled as to how he should correctly carry out his task of piloting her. He solved his dilemma by the semi-comic solution of shouting instructions at the top of his voice to Tom Healy who, as rider in attendance, kept pace with them both. Thus the Cheshire field was amused, though the Empress was not, to hear as the three of them approached a fence Rivers-Bulkeley shouting: 'Ride on at this one, Tom', or, 'Take a pull here, Tom'. It was a far cry indeed from the community of hand and spirit which had existed with Bay.

On the following day, to the astonishment of the suite, she announced that she was too tired to hunt and remained alone in her apartments. This was the first time in all the visits that she had voluntarily missed a day's hunting.

That evening Georg and Marie Larisch arrived in Whitchurch and were immediately summoned to Combermere. One can only conjecture what passed between Marie and the Empress when they retired for their customary gossip. No one knows, or will ever know, what was said but events make it a safe assumption that the Empress expressed her longing to hunt with Middleton again and that a message was sent to him to this effect. If Marie Larisch was the intermediary it was a position she had occupied on various occasions before.

On the threshold of his marriage Middleton might have been; he still could not keep away. He responded 'as a moth to the flame'. Risking the displeasure of the Bairds, the indignation of his fiancée and the stretching if not quite breaking of the rigid rules of his caste, he posted down to an hotel in Shropshire.

The North Shropshire Hounds met at Pries Station on the Monday of that week. Charles Kinsky, Rivers-Bulkeley, Marie and Georg Larisch with the Empress made up the party in her special train. As they joined the field a well-remembered figure detached itself from a group of riders, came forward and removed his hat. It was Bay Middleton. Those about her saw the Empress's face light up as she greeted him. Immediately Rivers-Bulkeley retired from his position as pilot and handed his charge over to Bay.

It was not a good day but they seemed so engrossed in each other's company that this hardly mattered. The following day he was out again and again they met, this time with the South Cheshire at Burley Dam, near where he had stationed his horses the previous year. This could not have been other than prearranged since without prior knowledge he could not have known with which of the many surrounding packs she intended to hunt that day. Once more Rivers-Bulkeley remained in the background and Bay piloted her.

It was evident to all how her demeanour changed when he was with her and how well she went in his company through a fast hunt of fifty-five minutes to ground near Wrenbury. There was now no need for instructions to be shouted at Healy. They were back in their perfect partnership again. Even the reporter from the local paper noticed the change in her. 'Her Majesty', he wrote, 'enjoyed the day's sport thoroughly.' It was the only time during this visit that he had occasion to record such words or any like them.

For tongues once more began to wag. The gossip inevitable in any hunting country, and especially where personages such as these were concerned, immediately started up again. Neither he nor she could afford any longer to be seen so openly in each other's company and enjoying it. The association, were it to continue, had to become a clandestine one and this did not suit the temperaments of either of them.

Yet the thought of losing him, especially now since she had met him and hunted with him again, must have wracked her. And the prospect of never seeing her again could not have been other than hell to him. She became once more listless, irritable and a creature of moods. She took to coming home early from hunting and to taking long walks alone, all actions quite out of character during a hunting visit. Moreover, when she did hunt it seemed to those about her that much of the old fire and dash had gone. A society paper commented on the fact that the ladies of Cheshire were universally down on her and held her reputation to be an exaggerated one. They said that she could not jump a fence by herself and that her skill in the saddle was much over-rated. 'How absurd to cry her up as a rider,' one of them said to the writer. 'Why, she cannot go without a pilot *and I can.*'

Middleton himself was going harder than ever both across the Shires and on the town. General Champion de Crespigny has told how his horses, whether hunting or racing, came back rowelled from the long cruel spurs everyone then wore and extraordinary tales of his doings in the night haunts of London began to circulate.

So both of them attempted to solve their separation in their own ways. But it was not then to become permanent. There was to be one more meeting. Bay was summoned to Combermere on the eve of her departure, and he came. The pretence, and it was a thin one, was that he was visiting friends in the locality and had called to pay his respects and to say goodbye.

The last dinner was a sentimental occasion. Only Marie Larisch, her cousin Heinrich, Rudi Liechtenstein, Middleton and the Empress sat down together.

Elizabeth wore a blue lilac-coloured *crêpe de chine* gown. She looked sad and lonely and lovely. Middleton sat at her right hand. While coffee was being served Marie sang to them 'The Last Rose of Summer'.

Afterwards the Empress left the table immediately and retired to her own apartments. Marie Larisch, going up to take her leave, found her shaken by sobs and almost hysterical. Tomorrow, she kept repeating, she would be back in captivity and this time there would be no release. 'Why can't I break my neck at a fence and end it all?' she demanded of her niece. She must have known then that she had indeed lost him and with him all hope of escape from the life she loathed so much.

Next morning as she waited for the carriages to take her to the train her mood was unchanged. Middleton was brought up to her apartments by Heinrich Larisch to take his own leave of her and to say farewell. He must have then repeated to her that his decision to marry was irrevocable and could not be reversed. She gave him a ring to remember her by and told him to keep it with him always.

The minutes flew by and neither of them appeared. The indoor servants were drawn up in two ranks in the hall to take their leave of her. Still she did not come down the great staircase. Heinrich Larisch prowled about, constantly looking at his watch. The time for the departure of the train was rapidly approaching. An audience with Queen Victoria at Windsor had been fixed for that afternoon, although the Empress was unlikely to care very much about what others might suffer if the appointment was not kept.

At length Larisch could wait no longer. He mounted the staircase and went towards the private apartments. In a few moments he returned with Middleton beside him. Bay was looking for once visibly shaken as if he had passed through a shattering emotional storm. The carriages were brought to the door but still the Empress did not reappear.

Then there was a slight stir in the hall and everyone looked up. In a black travelling costume trimmed with fur, a small black hat on her piled auburn tresses she stood for a moment with her hand on the newel post. She looked, as her niece, after all the years of bitterness and recrimination that had passed between them, could not help remembering and recording, every inch an Empress.

Coming down the staircase she walked between the servants—one wonders what they thought—with a charming word for each. The butler and housekeeper received jewelled tokens and Lord Combermere was presented with a gold snuff-box, elaborately chased with a crown and the letter E set in diamonds on the lid.

The outdoor staff lined the drive. They, too, were graciously thanked. MacDonald and Healy were brought forward and after she had given them her special word of thanks they were told to sell all her horses at Tattersalls in Rugby as soon as it could be arranged. This alone indicates her recognition of the finality of it all and that hunting without Bay was not hunting at all. Then she entered the carriage to be driven to the station.

Middleton and Heinrich Larisch followed in another carriage. As the train pulled out from the station, Middleton stood a little apart from the others on the platform and watched it carry her out of his life forever.

They never saw each other again. She never again rode to hounds in England.

They had played their parts in their strange romance according to their lights and the rules and orders of their caste and kind and played them well. Those six years of separation and encounter, excitement, endeavour and companionship, had given her a glimpse of happiness if never true fulfilment. Being what she was she did not give a thought to those other things those years might have done—the wrecking of Rudolph's life through their estrangement and the driving of him into hasty loves and a loveless marriage; the effect on Anglo-Irish affairs; and the deep damage to relations between the English and Austro-Hungarian ruling houses. For her, as always, it was a dream life, a glimpse of what she might have had and done had she remained the private person she always wished to be. It was, then, an apt epitaph to it all that as the train drew out she turned to her companion and said: 'Play-acting, my dear child, is the sad lot of those who wear a crown.'

Epilogue

What happened to them all?

After she left England in 1882 Elizabeth had a few days hunting in France and then went out a few times at Gödollo. But the fun and the fire of it were both missing in Bay's absence. Soon she ceased to hunt and a little later gave up riding altogether. Long walks at a great pace and sometimes lasting for seven or eight hours were substituted as exercise and as a means of preserving her figure. She cut her diet to a minimum and existed mostly on milk. Melancholy and restlessness possessed her. 'His dark Majesty is my constant companion', she recorded in her commonplace book.

She did not, however, forget her horses and the joyful days she had on them with Bay in England and Ireland. Her 'riding chapel' was preserved and the portraits by Richter and others, including all the horses she had hunted in Cheshire, were hung on its walls. Here she would sit for hours silently gazing at their pictures, old memories and half-forgotten excitements and delights coming crowding back to her. Only a few friends were admitted to this room. One of them was Marion Gilbert to whom she said: 'I have lost all these friends and have never gained one. Many have gone to their death for me which no man has ever done: they would rather assassinate me.'

Distress and emergency, however, could still call out the best in her. During the Mayerling tragedy and the ensuing scandal her public conduct and courage were exemplary and gained her the admiration even of those at court who disliked and disapproved of her. But this terrible ordeal followed shortly by the deaths of Andrassy and her sister, Nene, brought on a *crise des nerfs* from which she never really recovered. In 1890 she embarked on a series of incessant wanderings. Corfu, where the extraordinary Achilleion Palace was built by her, formed at first a refuge. 'I am too old to struggle. My wings have been singed and now all I long for is rest.' But she was only fifty and rest she could not find.

In 1898 her wanderings brought her to the Beau Rivage Hotel in Geneva. Unknown to her a young anarchist, Luchini, with a spirit almost as strange and tortured as her own, had arrived at the same place. 'How I should like to kill somebody; but it must be some person of great importance, so that it might get into the papers', he told a friend. The 'person of importance' he appears to have selected seems to have been either the Duke of Orleans or the Duke of Chartres, both of whom were expected in Geneva. They did not come, however, and instead the newspapers, though requested to observe her incognito, were full of the arrival and presence of the Empress in the city. On 10 September she decided to leave by boat for Caux. Luchini, who had kept her hotel under observation, followed her when she left it. A little distance away from the quayside, where there were few bystanders, he caught up with her and drove his weapon—a dagger improvised from a file—into her breast. Elizabeth fell to the ground. She regained her feet almost immediately, however, and with her extraordinary vitality, walked on to the boat. There she collapsed. She was borne back to the hotel where she died in a few minutes. The tip of the dagger had only just pierced her heart. In death she looked happy. Her youth appeared to have come back to her face and with it her spring-like loveliness. There was a slight smile on her lips.

Luchini had served for a short time in the Austrian Army. By an irony of fate which she would perhaps have enjoyed, the soldierly qualities for which he had received his highest recommendation were 'riding and jumping'.

Bay Middleton was married to Charlotte Baird on Thursday, 26 October 1882 at St George's, Hanover Square. Parson Drake, the famous fox-hunting parson, came especially from the West Country to assist at the ceremony. Middleton gave his address as 27 Half Moon Street, his flat in town.

The bride was said to bring to her husband an income of £20,000 a year; she was also said to have been exceedingly jealous of the Empress and would allow no mention of her name in her presence. Certainly she destroyed all the correspondence and the perishable mementoes, but the stock-pin of diamonds surrounding the Imperial E, the locket and the cuff-links were —and are—preserved, as was the ring which Bay kept always with him.

His brilliance as a rider to hounds remained unsurpassed; his successes in point-to-point and hunt races continued unchecked. Oddly enough he never had a mount in the Grand National, the winning of which was the ambition of every amateur rider in those days, nor did he ever succeed in winning the Grand National Hunt Steeplechase, the 'Amateur's Grand National'. His feats on Lord of the Harem have already been mentioned. Baker Pasha, Midsummer, Punjaub and Doneraile were other good horses he owned and on which he ran up a series of victories.

As he became older his deafness increased and with it his fits of melancholia and his consuming premonition that he was destined to die early and violently.

At the beginning of the point-to-point season of 1892, when visiting Dublin, he lost the ring which the Empress had given him. This upset him terribly and his premonition of an approaching sudden death became more pronounced. As the season progressed he told Sir Herbert Langham that he was convinced he would be killed in the next few days. A friend, Captain Riddell, hearing this, went to Bay and advised him to give up riding races. He was then forty-six and, Riddell pointed out, had been taking too many chances for too long. Bay's reply was that he wanted to win the Midland Sportsman's Cup to be run for at the House of Commons meeting at Kineton the following week and that after that he would retire.

He stayed for the meeting with Mr Ernest Cassel, the financier and friend of the Prince of Wales, who gave a house party at Compton Verney for it. Sir Chandos Leigh, who was amongst the guests, noticed that Bay seemed very subdued and in the grip of a depression he appeared unable to shake off. After dinner Bay came to Sir Chandos's room and they talked together until one o'clock in the morning. He was, Sir Chandos says, 'very depressed and melancholy and talked of nothing but cricket'.

When the horses were brought round to be ridden to the meeting, Bay bade Mrs Cassel goodbye and told her that for the first time in his life he wished he was going in the carriage. Chandos Leigh and he rode together to the course. Leigh had judged at a number of meetings that season and he was to judge the House of Commons race at this one. After it was over Lord Willoughby de Broke came to him and asked him to judge the Sportsman's Cup. He agreed to do so and as he hurried to get the numbers and details he wanted he spoke to Bay who was just going out. He was the last of his friends ever to do so.

What appears to have happened in the race, though no one has ever been able to say with complete certainty, is that when the riders turned for home and began to cram on the pace Bay, on Night Line, was lying well up. Not far from the finish was a fence consisting of a rail with a drop into a ridge and furrow field beyond it. Here Night Line pecked badly. Bay went forward. As he did so, the horse, trying to recover, threw up his head. The poll took Bay on the point of his chin and broke his neck. He was dead before he hit the ground.

He was buried at Haselbech in full hunting costume. Two of his friends placed an inscribed granite block at the place where he was killed. Lord Willoughby de Broke had a fence erected round it and the enclosure planted. His death threw the whole sporting world into the deepest gloom. No one ever knew what the Empress thought. She was off on her strange, almost crazed wanderings when it happened. If she wrote, the letter was destroyed with the rest.

Many tributes to him were written and a few lines of one of them deserves quoting. Harry Bentley, a very minor hunting poet, had along with Ernest Cassel, Frank Mildmay MP and others, ridden in the race himself. He composed a long eulogy much of which is florid and sentimental but these lines ring true:

> And we shall miss you at the covert-side,
> Or when the hounds are drawing Scotland wood,
> Or go away with breast-high scent we still
> Shall miss the gallant figure leading us
> In the quick burst across the Cottesbrooke Vale,

Or at the meeting where the oft-heard cry
Rings out no more, 'Bay wins on Doneraile!'

Leonard Morrogh retired from the Mastership of the Ward hounds in the middle eighties. He then purchased a property at Sleedagh in County Wexford and from there continued to hunt with the Killinick Harriers and the Wexford Hounds. In January 1889 when out with the latter pack, as usual amongst the first few in a fast hunt, a concealed strand of wire in a fence turned his horse over on top of him. Both his legs were broken and his spine badly injured. Captain Maher of Ballinkeele, the owner of Frigate, who was to win the Grand National that year, was the first at his side. On Maher's instructions Morrogh was taken to the nearest house which was Castleboro, the seat of Lord Carew. There Morrogh died three days later. He was buried in Glasnevin, County Dublin. The ubiquitous Colonel Forster, who was still Master of the Horse at Dublin Castle, represented the Lord Lieutenant and virtually the whole of hunting Ireland turned out to mourn him.

Thus the two most favoured amongst her friends and pilots came to sudden and tragic ends in the sports they and she loved so well within a year or so of each other and not many years before her own assassination.

As to Spencer, his further career was strange indeed. On Gladstone's accession to the Premiership in 1882 he was appointed Lord Lieutenant of Ireland for a second term. Hardly had he been sworn in than the Phoenix Park Murders took place. Lord Frederick Cavendish, the Chief Secretary, and Mr Burke, the Under Secretary, were done to death almost at the gates of the Viceregal Lodge.

During this viceroyalty Spencer became an ardent advocate of Gladstonian conciliation and of Home Rule for Ireland. As a result he was held by most, if not all, of his former friends amongst the nobility and gentry to have turned his coat. He forfeited their friendship and earned instead their detestation. There was an attempt to horse-whip him by the wife of one of these, and at a reception when he was suffering from lumbago and placing his hands on his back another remarked, 'that is only His Excellency feeling for his backbone'. On account of these policies he also forfeited what little royal favour was left to him as a result of his association with the Empress. It is said, and with authority, that had the Queen asked Gladstone for his advice on a successor in 1894 he would have named Spencer. It is also said that she knew this very well, which was the reason for her not taking counsel with the retiring premier and sending on her own authority for Rosebery.

Spencer's policy in Ireland was unquestionably the right one but his manner of adopting it was, as might be expected from his character, peremptory and autocratic so that it at least gave the appearance of a betrayal of his former convictions and friends. Kipling in 1891 wrote a savage attack on him in 'The Ballad of the Red Earl' which, like others of Kipling's attacks, was almost certainly libellous but which Spencer had either the good sense or Olympian detachment to ignore. He certainly earned the execrations of many of his fellows in society. Walpurga Lady Paget, admittedly a high Tory but also one of Queen Victoria's closest personal friends, wrote of him: 'Mr Gladstone's great power lies in his never reading a paper, but I blame him far less than Lords Granville, Hartington and Spencer, who destroy their country that they may remain in office.'

After 1894 Spencer did not hold office again and gradually withdrew from public life. His last Mastership of the Pytchley also did not end happily, with the appointment of a committee which could act as a curb on his despotic powers. His income had suffered during the agricultural depression which caused him to sell the great library at Althorp and dispose of his oriental manuscripts. He died in 1910.

Crown Prince Rudolph who saw, if only darkly and through a miasma of personal dissipation and marital disaster, that the Empire was heading for collapse, tried to do something to change the course of events. It was little enough that he could do. His mother had to all intents and purposes retired from court and society; his father ignored him, allowing him neither sight of state papers nor any say in government. Thus he was driven to propagating such liberal views as he had through journalism or long letters to Szeps in which he kept the editor informed of inside knowledge of what was happening in the governing corridors of the Hofburg. But soon frustration, disease, dissipation and his heredity all began to wreak havoc with his constitution and his mind.

In January 1889 he brought Mary Vetsera, daughter of Baroness Vetsera and niece of the Baltazzi brothers, to his hunting lodge at Mayerling. There he shot first her and, after an appreciable interval, himself. Owing to the efforts of the Emperor and his advisers to have all news of the matter suppressed, the wildest rumours of assassination, duels and murder flew around Europe. Some of them still survive; nevertheless, all the evidence points unequivocally to suicide, especially since shortly before the tragedy Rudolph had approached another woman with a suicide pact.

On Franz Joseph's orders the hunting lodge was demolished and a Carmelite convent erected in its place. The high altar of the chapel now stands on the very spot formerly occupied by the bed where the bodies lay until discovered by Rudolph's valet. All that remains of the original structure is the 'tea-pavilion' in the garden.

Rudolph's body lies alongside those of his parents in a special vault in the crypt of the Capuchin Chapel on the Neumarkt in Vienna. Someone still remembers him. When the writer visited there recently a red rose lay on his coffin lid.

Those who were close to Franz Joseph and those few who now recall him refer to him as a great gentleman and, with all his faults, they are right. A shy, reserved man of great physical and moral courage he was courteous, thoughtful and considerate to all. Unfortunately these latter qualities were tempered by neither sympathy nor understanding. They sprang not from his nature but from his training and his enormous innate sense of his duties and responsibilities. His qualities of courage and endurance and his Habsburg lineage made him unable to compel himself to bend to any of the many storms that beset him during his long life. He had to face them four square and see them out. The result was that in the end they wrecked him and brought his Empire tumbling down.

He was also both in his public and private life the unluckiest monarch of the century. His son committed a gaudy suicide, his wife withdrew from him into a life of neurotic fantasy. His heir, from whom he was estranged, was assassinated at Sarajevo. Both events and those nearest to him betrayed and disappointed him. He did find for a short time some sort of domestic consolation in the company of Frau Schratt but even she could not compete with the Habsburg combination of preoccupation with self and slavery to duty and she left.

'Is nothing to be spared me?' was his despairing cry when they brought him the news of Sisi's assassination. Then, Prince Clary has told the author, he added under his breath in a voice so low that the equerry could hardly catch the words he may in any event have not been intended to hear: 'No one will ever know how much I loved her.'

Marie Larisch could resist neither money nor intrigue. She became much involved with Baroness Vetsera and her daughter. It was she who acted as intermediary between Rudolph and Mary Vetsera and she actually escorted the girl to Rudolph's apartments in the Hofburg before the last journey to Mayerling. There is evidence to show that she was desperately in debt at this time and that Rudolph paid her for these services. After the tragedy an incriminating letter was found in the pocket of one of Rudolph's tunics which he had given to a painter who was then engaged in making a formal portrait of him. The painter sent the letter to the Emperor. In addition, in Rudolph's 'dying disposition', a reference was made to letters from Marie Larisch which he instructed were to be destroyed. This led court officials to them and provided further evidence of her involvement in the affair.

The Empress, torn by grief and guilt, was shocked and horrified to learn of the part her former favourite and confidante had played in the scandal. Marie Larisch was banned from her presence forever and she and her husband cast into virtual exile. The marriage did not prosper and in 1896 they were divorced.

In 1897 Marie married again but this marriage was unsuccessful also. Count Corti says that her son by her first marriage committed suicide after reading a newspaper article describing the part played by his mother in Mayerling. In 1913 an English ghost writer collaborated with her in a book of memoirs aimed at justifying her actions and her part in the Mayerling tragedy. She was then living at Metz almost in squalor and her appearance had greatly deteriorated. Later she emigrated to America and married for a third time. Here she published two other volumes of memoirs, also ghosted. These succeeded in rescuing her temporarily from financial distress.

The books, as Corti says, are an unreliable mixture of truth and fiction. They are also inspired in places by a considerable animus against her former benefactress, the Empress. Nevertheless, the fact remains that she did know more than anyone, save possibly Countess Festetics, of what went on in the Empress's mind and in her private life during the period she was close to her. Certain facts as to dates and visits and the like which can be checked against published lists come out as surprisingly accurate, just as certain of the wilder stories can be easily dismissed. The tragedy is that the books, especially the later ones, were written for popular consumption and serialisation and little effort seems to have been made to treat them as the raw material of history, which they were, and to sift the self-justification and scandalous 'revelations' from the truth.

Charles Kinsky became in due course Prince Kinsky and head of that great house. He won the Grand National on his own mare Zoedone in 1883. He had first seen her at the Ash Hunt Meeting in Cheshire which he attended with Middleton and the Empress. Middleton advised him to buy her then but he did not do so until the following year. As he passed the post a winner the first thing he heard was Middleton's 'view holloa' shouting him home. He continued to ride in and win many races in Austria, Hungary, Paris and England and to hunt in the Shires. On one occasion at Sandown he had a bad fall at the open ditch ending up with a broken nose and arm, all the skin off his face and his horse on top of him. One of his friends tried to pull him out by the broken arm. Roddy Owen, one of the greatest riders and characters ever to grace the racecourse, who had also fallen at that fence, afterwards remarked to a friend: 'The fellow may be an Austrian Count but he swears in English even better than I do!'

Kinsky married in 1895 Countess Elizabeth von Wolff-Metternich, but for years he nursed a hopeless passion for Lady Randolph Churchill. An Englishman by adoption, he was elected to the National Hunt Committee and made an honorary member of the Jockey Club in 1906. Branded an enemy alien at the beginning of the Great War, he died a year or so later—of a broken heart, or so it was said.

Bibliography

Apsley, Lady *To Whom the Goddess* (London, 1932)

Bailey's Hunting Directory (London, various volumes)
Barkeley, Richard *The Road to Mayerling* (London, 1958)
Beust, Count *Memoirs* (two vols) (London, 1887)
Blake, Robert *Disraeli* (London, 1966)
Blew, C. W. A. *History of Steeplechasing* (London, 1901)
Brindley, Jim *Reminiscences and Rhymes of The Ward Hunt* (Dublin, 1923)
British Hunts and Huntsmen Vols 1–4 (London, 1908–1911)
de Burgh, A. *Elisabeth Empress of Austria* (London, 1898)

Carlisle, R. H. *Fox-Hunting Past and Present* (London, 1908)
Cassels, Lavender *Clash of Generations* (London, 1973)
Corballis, J. H. *Forty-Five Years of Sport* (London, 1891)
Corfe, Tom *The Phoenix Park Murders* (London, 1968)
Corti, Count Egon *Elizabeth Empress of Austria* (London, 1936)
Der Alte Kaiser (Vienna, 1955)
Cowles, Virginia *Edward VII and His Circle* (London, 1956)
Crankshaw, Edward *The Fall of the House of Habsburg* (London, 1963)
The Habsburgs (London, 1971)
de Crespigny, Sir Claude Champion *Forty Years of a Sportsman's Life* (London, 1910)

Davenport, Henry S. *Memories at Random, Melton and Harborough* (London, 1926)

Elliott, J. M. K. *Fifty Years of Hunting with the Grafton and Other Packs* (London, 1900)

Fleury, Maurice *Memoirs of The Empress Elizabeth*
Frewen, Moreton *Melton Mowbray and Other Memories* (London, n.d.)
Fugger, Princess *The Glory of the Habsburgs* (London, 1932)
Fulford, Roger (Ed.) *Dearest Mama* Letters. 1861–1864

Gilbert, Marion *Elizabeth de Wittelsbach* (Paris, 1932)
Graham, Sir Reginald, Bt. *Foxhunting Recollections* (London, 1908)
Greaves, Ralph *A Short History of the Ward Union Hounds* (Dublin, n.d.)
Gribble, Francis. *Life of the Emperor Francis Joseph* (London, 1914)

Harding, Bertita *Golden Fleece* (New York, 1937)
Haslip, Joan *The Lonely Empress* (London, 1965)

Judtmann, Fritz *Mayerling, The Facts Behind The Legend* (London, 1971)

Ketterl, Eugen *Emperor Franz Josef I* (London, 1929)
Kurtz, Harold *The Empress Eugenie* (London, 1964)

Larisch, Countess Marie *My Past* (London, 1913)
Secrets of a Royal House (London, 1935)
My Royal Relatives (London, 1936)
Leigh, Sir Chandos *Bar, Bat and Bit* (London, 1913)
Leslie, Anita *Edwardians in Love* (London, 1972)
Longford, Elizabeth *Victoria R.I.* (London, 1964)
Longay, Count Carl *Rudolph—The Tragedy of Mayerling* (London, 1950)

McDowell, R. B. *The Irish Administration, 1801–1814* (London, 1964)
Magnus, Sir Philip *Edward VII* (London, 1964)
Mason, Finch *Heroes and Heroines of the Grand National* (London, 1911)
Margutti, Lieut-Gen. Baron von *The Emperor Franz Joseph and His Times* (London, 1921)
Melton Rough-Rider, A. *Rum 'Uns to Follow. Memories of Seventy Years in the Shires* (London, 1934)
Bad 'Uns to Beat (London, 1936)

de Montmorency, Hervey *Sword and Stirrup* (London, 1936)
Mordaunt, Sir Charles and Verney, W. R. *Annals of the Warwickshire Hunt 1795–1895* (2 Vols) (London, 1896)
Morris, M. O'Connor *Hibernica Hippica* (London, 1900)

Nethercote, H. O. *The Pytchley Hunt Past and Present* (London, 1888)

O'Broin, Leon *Fenian Fever* (London, 1971)
O'Donoghue, Mrs Power *Ladies on Horseback* (London, 1896)
O'Mahony, Charles *The Viceroys of Ireland* (London, 1912)
Owen, Margaret Cunliffe *The Martyrdom of an Empress* (London, 1899)

Paget, Guy *The History of the Althorp and Pytchley Hunt* (London, 1937)
Paget, J. Otho *Memories of the Shires* (London, 1920)
Paget, Walpurga, Lady *Embassies of Other Days* (2 Vols) (London, 1923)
The Linings of Life (2 Vols) (London, 1928)
Pennell-Elmhirst, E. *The Best Season on Record* (London, 1885)
The Cream of Leicestershire. Eleven Seasons' Skimmings (London, 1883)
The Best of the Fun (London, 1903)
Pearsall, Ronald *The Worm in the Bud* (London, 1969)
Ponsonby, Sir Frederick, first Lord Sysonby *Recollections of Three Reigns* (London, 1951)
Powell, Lady Violet *A Very Substantial Ghost* (London, 1967)
Portland, The Duke of *Memoirs of Racing and Hunting* (London, 1935)
Men, Women and Things (London, 1937)

Radziwill, Princess Catherine *The Austrian Court from Within* (London, 1916)
Richardson J. M. and Finch Mason *Gentlemen Riders Past and Present* (London, 1909)
Rossmore, Lord *Things I Can Tell* (London, 1912)

Sargent, H. S. *Thoughts on Sport* (London, 1895)

Taylor, A. J. P. *The Habsburg Monarchy* (London, 1941)
Thormanby *Kings of the Hunting Field* (London, 1899)

Sporting Stories (London, n.d.)
Tschuppik, Carl *Empress Elisabeth of Austria* (London, 1930)

Voigt, C. A. *Famous Gentlemen Riders at Home and Abroad* (London, n.d.)

Ward, Leslie *Forty Years of Spy* (London, 1915)
Watson, S. *Between the Flags, A History of Irish Steeplechasing* (Dublin, 1969)
Whitehurst, F. F. *Tallyho* (London, 1878)
Wyndham, Col. the Hon. H. *The Pytchley Mastership of the Fifth Earl Spencer* (Kettering, 1970)

Yates, Arthur *Arthur Yates, Trainer and Gentleman Rider* (London, 1924)

Periodicals and Magazines

Baily's Magazine
Bell's Life
Cheshire Advertiser
Country Gentleman
Field
Field of Ireland
Freeman's Journal
Graphic
Horse and Hound
Illustrated London News
Illustrated Sporting and Dramatic News
Irish Times
Isle of Wight Express
Life
Leicester Journal
Liverpool Echo
Liverpool Daily Courier
Morning Post
Northampton Herald
Northampton Mercury
Queen
Racing Calendar
Sporting Life
Sportsman
Sporting Times
The Times
Truth
Vanity Fair
World

Index